MILITARY LAW LEXICON

MILITARY LAW LEXICON

By

Maj Gen Nilendra Kumar

Judge Advocate General (Army)

and

Kush Chaturvedi

Universal
Law Publishing Co. Pvt. Ltd.

2006 Edition

ISBN : 81-7534-573-X

Published by
UNIVERSAL LAW PUBLISHING CO. PVT. LTD.
C-FF-1A, Dilkhush Industrial Estate,
(Opp. Hans Cinema, Azadpur) G.T. Karnal Road,
Delhi-110 033
Tel : 011-27438103, 27215334, 42381334
Fax : 011-27458529
E-mail *(For sales inquiries)* : sales@unilawbooks.com
E-mail *(For editorial inquiries)* : edit@unilawbooks.com
Website : www.unilawbooks.com

Recommended citation: *Military Law Lexicon*, Maj Gen Nilendra Kumar and Kush Chaturvedi (New Delhi: Universal Law Publishing Co. Pvt. Ltd., 2006)

Computer Typeset at Aesthetic & *Printed at* Mudrak , New Delhi.

This Work is dedicated to
Rekha, Neha & Nishith

FOREWORD

Precision and clarity of terminology is a prime consideration in communication and the need for correct and effective use of terms in the affairs of military legal practice and security jurisprudence can never be over emphasized. This is because the subject is directly associated with aspects such as discipline of men in uniform, their life, liberty, legality of use of force and laws of war. The actual connotation and implication of each term used is, therefore, required to be clearly known and understood by all practitioners of military law.

The book reflects the painstaking effort of the authors whose extensive research of diverse military literature has culminated in a comprehensive compendium of military law lexicon and which is no doubt a unique initiative. I am sanguine that it will be of immense use to all students and practitioners of military law.

(JJ Singh)
General

21 Jul 2006

PREFACE

In the present times, awareness about defence related strategic issues has increased manifold. More than ever before, the public at large seeks to be abreast of matters concerning defence. Just as interest in military law has been on the rise, similarly growing desire to understand laws in their various contexts is clearly visible. However, a lack of comprehending the unique military legal system impedes the study of military matters. Particular words, which are commonly used, often acquire a specific meaning in military law parlance. Moreover, there are certain terms which are unique to military law which should be properly understood.

The authors have tried here to rectify the lacunae by bringing out a lexicon of military legal terms which they hope will be a first step for understanding military terms which a majority of the public is not familiar with. It is an endeavour to assimilate a comprehensive list of terms which are frequently used in military legal publications. For a fuller comprehension, the terms have been explained by a combination of means *i.e.,* sometimes by their dictionary meaning or by statutory definitions and at places by a combination of both. While the basic focus is on an understanding of words and terms as relevant under Indian statutory laws, for greater relevance, terms of foreign usage have also been included. The addition of law maxims relevant to the subject and an alphabetical catalogue of abbreviations have been incorporated for easy reference.

As no such publication is currently available, we hope that this work will clear the misty and sometimes incomprehensible military legal literature for the uninitiated and will be a useful aid to Military law practitioners, students, law enforcement officials, security experts, media personnel, court officials, together with members of the public who seek to educate themselves about this specialised field.

We express our sincere thanks to Sri BK Tewari whose help for this book was invaluable. Rekha and Neha have greatly assisted us with the corrections and our profound thanks to them. Further we acknowledge the keen interest and support provided by the Publishers and specially Sri Manish Arora.

01 October 2006 **Authors**

PREFACE

In the present times, awareness about defence related strategic issues has increased manifold. More than ever before, the public at large seeks to be abreast of matters concerning defence. Just as interest in military law has been on the rise, similarly, growth, desire to understand laws in their various contexts is clearly visible. However, a lack of comprehending the unique military legal words, impedes the study of military matters. Particular words, which are commonly used, often acquire a specific meaning in military law parlance. Moreover, there are certain terms which are unique to military law, which should be properly understood.

The authors have tried here to rectify the inadequacy by bringing out a lexicon of military legal terms which they hope will be a first step for laymen [illegible] military terms which are a rarity to the public. It is not a dictionary but it is an endeavour to assimilate a [illegible] of terms which are frequently used in military legal publications, [illegible]. The terms have been explained by a combination of meanings – sometimes by their dictionary meaning or by statutory definitions and at places by a combination of both. While the basic focus is on an [illegible] of words and terms as relevant under Indian [illegible] [illegible] [illegible] category.

As no such publication is currently available, we hope that this work will clear the misty and sometime incomprehensible military legal literature for the uninitiated and will be a useful aid to Military law practitioners, students, law enforcement officials, security experts, media personnel, court officials, together with members of the public who seek to educate themselves about this specialised field.

We express our sincere thanks to Smt. K. Tewari whose help for this book was invaluable. Rekha and Neha have greatly assisted us with the corrections and our profound thanks to them. Further we acknowledge the keen interest and support provided by the Publishers and specially Sri Manish Arora.

01 October 2006 **Authors**

CONTENTS

CONTENTS

ABBREVIATIONS AND ACRONYMS

AA	Army Act
AAO	Area Accounts Office
AAP	Annual Acquisition Plan
AC	Appeal Cases
ACR	Annual Confidential Report
ADC	Army Dental Corps/Aide de Camp
ADG	Additional Director General
AEC	Army Education Corps
AF(SP)A	Armed Forces (Special Powers) Act
AG	Adjutant General
AI	Army Instructions
AMC	Army Medical Corps
ANC	Andaman & Nicobar Command
AO	Army Order/Accounts Officer
AOC	Army Ordnance Corps
AOR	Area of Responsibility
AON	Acceptance of Necessity
AP	Additional Protocol
APO	Army Purchase Organisation/Army Post Office
AR	Army Rules
ASC	Army Service Corps
AT	Acceptance of Tender
ATN	Action Taken Notes
AU	African Union
AVM	Anti-Vehicle Landmine/Air Vice Marshal
AWHO	Army Welfare Housing Organisation
AWOL	Absent without Leave
BCN	Biological, Chemical and Nuclear
BIO	Bulk Inspection Officer
CA	Civil Affairs

CAAF	Court of Appeal for the Armed Forces
CAB	Complaint Advisory Board
CAS	Chief of the Air Staff
CBM	Confidence Building Measure
CCS	Cabinet Committee on Security
CCW	Convention on Certain Conventional Weapons
CD	Conference on Disarmament/Counter Drug
CDA	Controller of Defence Accounts
CDP	Chief Director Purchase
CFA	Competent Financial Authority
CGDA	Controller General of Defence Accounts
CI	Counter Insurgency/Counter Intelligence
CIA	Central Intelligence Agency
CICC	Coalition for the International Criminal Court
CIDS	Chief of the Integrated Defence Staff
CIMC	Civil Military Cooperation
C-IN-C	Commander-in-Chief
CIPA	Classified Information Procedures Act
CISC	Chief of Integrated Staff Committee
CISF	Central Industrial Security Force
CJA	Command Judge Advocate
CKD	Completely Knocked Down
CLA	Chief Legal Adviser
CM	Court-Martial
CMAC	Court-Martial Appeal Court
CMOC	Civil Military Operations Centre
CNC	Contract Negotiating Committee
CNS	Chief of the Naval Staff
CO	Commanding Officer
COAS	Chief of the Army Staff

C of I	Court of Inquiry
COTS	Commercially off the Shelf
Cr PC	Criminal Procedure·Code
CPA	Coalition Provisional Authority
CPMP	The Military Criminal Code for Peace Time (Italy)
CPO	Central Police Organisations
CPR	Conceptual Project Report
CQA	Close Quarter Assassination
CR	Character Roll/Confidential Report
CRO	Crisis Response Operations/Civilian Relief Operations
CSD	Canteen Stores Department
CST	Comparative Statement of Tenders
CT	Counter Terrorism
CTBT	Comprehensive Test Ban Treaty
CTF	Combined Task Force
CWC	Chemical Weapons Convention
DAC	Defence Acquisition Council
DAE	Department of Atomic Energy
DC	Defence Counsel
DCM	District Court-Martial
DDP	Department of Defence Production
DEO	Defence Estate Officer
DG	Director General
DG ADS	Director General Audit Defence Services
DG DE	Director General Defence Estates
DI	Dispatch Instructions
DLS	Directorate of Legal Services
DNA	Damage and Needs Assessment
DOD	Department of Defence
DODD	Department of Defence Directive
DOJ	Department of Justice
DP	Delivery Period
DPC	Departmental Promotion Committee

DPP	Defence Procurement Procedure
DPR	Detailed Project Report
DRI	Directorate of Revenue Intelligence
DSR	Defence Service Regulations
DV	Discipline & Vigilance
EA	Electronic Attack
EAR	Export Administration Regulations (USA)
EC	Emergency Commission
ECHR	European Convention on Human Rights
EEA	Export Administration Act, 1979 (of USA)
EEZ	Exclusive Economic Zone
ERE	Extra Regimental Employment
ERW	Explosive Remnants of War
ESL	Estimated Shelf Life
ESP	Engineering Support Package
EU	European Union
FBI	Federal Bureau of Investigation
FBR	Fast Breeder Reactors
FCA	Foreign Claims Act
FDI	Foreign Direct Investment
FEMA	Federal Emergency Management Agency
FIO	Food Inspection Organisation
FISA	Foreign Intelligence Surveillance Act (of 1978)
FISCR	Foreign Intelligence Surveillance Court of Review
FPN	Final Performance Notice
GA	General Assembly (United Nations)
GBV	Gender Based Violence
GC	Geneva Conventions/Gentleman Cadet
GCM	General Court-Martial
GJA	Group Judge Advocate
GOC	General Officer Commanding

GOC-in-C	General Officer Commanding-in-Chief
GOI	Government of India
GRDI	Global Retail Development Index
GWOT	Global War on Terrorism
HN	Host Nation
HOC	Humanitarian Operations Centre
HQ	Headquarters
HRL	Human Rights Law
IAEA	International Atomic Energy Agency
IC	Indian Commission
ICC	International Criminal Court
ICE	Immigration & Customs Enforcement
ICJ	International Court of Justice
ICRC	International Committee of the Red Cross
ICTR	International Criminal Tribunal for Rwanda
ICTY	International Criminal Tribunal for the Former Yugoslavia
IDS	Integrated Defence Staff
IEEPA	International Emergency Economic Powers Act (USA)
IEA	Indian Evidence Act
IFA	Integrated Financial Advisor
IHL	International Humanitarian Law
IMB	International Maritime Bureau
IMDG	International Maritime Dangerous Goods Code
IML	Institute of Military Law
IMO	International Maritime Organisation
IO	Investigating Officer
IPC	Indian Penal Code
ISAF	International Security Assistance Force
JA	Judge Advocate

JAG	Judge Advocate General
JC	Junior Commission
JCO	Junior Commissioned Officer
JCS	Joint Chiefs of Staff
JIC	Joint Interrogation Centre
JSQR	Joint Services Qualitative Requirement
KIA	Killed in Action
LCA	Logistics Capability Assessment
LE	Law Enforcement
LEA	Law Enforcement Authority/Agencies
LOAC	Law of Armed Conflicts
LOC	Line of Control
LOSC	Law of Sea Convention
LRIT	Long Range Identification and Tracking (of ships)
LTIPP	Long Term Integrated Perspective Plan
LTPP	Long Term Perspective Plan
MCC	Military Criminal Code
MCM	Manual for Court-Martial
MCS	Monitoring Control and Surveillance System
MCT	Military Critical Technologies
MEH	Marine Electronic Highway
MES	Military Engineering Service
MIA	Missing in Action
MI	Military Intelligence
MIML	Manual of Indian Military Law
MIO	Maritime Interception Operations
MISPO	Marketing Intelligence and Statistics Processing Officer
MJ	Military Judge
MLAT	Mutual Legal Assistance Treaty
Mil LJ	Military Law Journal

MML	Manual of Military Law
MNF	Multi National Force
MNS	Military Nursing Service
MOD	Ministry of Defence
MOOTW	Military Operations Other Than War
MOTR	Maritime Operational Threat Response
MOU	Memorandum of Understanding
MP	Military Police
MRE	Military Rules of Evidence
MS	Military Secretary
MTCR	Missile Technology Control Regime
NCC	National Cadet Corps
NCIS	Naval Criminal Investigation Service
NCNC	No Cost – No Commitment
NCO	Non Commissioned Officer
NDA	National Defence Academy
NEA	National Emergency Act (USA)
NEO	Non-Combatants Evacuation Operations
NIT	Notice Inviting Tender
NNWS	Non Nuclear Weapon State
NPT	Non Proliferation Treaty
NR	Not Recommended
NSA	National Security Adviser
NSG	Nuclear Supplier's Group/National Security Guard
NYR	Not Yet Recommended
OACOs	Out of Area Combined Operations
OC	Officer Commanding/Organized Crime
OCC	Operational Code of Conduct
OCHA	UN Office for the Coordination in Human Affairs
OEM	Original Equipment Manufacturers
OFC	Overall Force Commander
OGA	Other Governmental Agency

OHR	Office of High Representative
OPCW	Organisation for the Prohibition of Chemical Weapons
OSC	On Scene Commander
OSL	Over Stayal of Leave
PA	Production Agency/Public Affairs/ Personal Assistant
P&A Regs	Pay and Allowances Regulations
PBG	President's Body Guard
PCDA	Principal Controller of Defence Accounts
PGM	Precision Guided Missile
PIC	Public Information Campaign
PKF	Peace Keeping Force
PKOs	Peace Keeping Operations
PMG	Peace Monitoring Group
PO	Peace Operations
PoW	Prisoner of War
PR	Price Reduction
PRC	Piracy Reporting Centre
PSI	Proliferation Security Initiative
PSO	Principal Staff Officer/Personal Servant of
PSOs	Peace Support Operations
QA	Quality Assurance
QB	Queen's Bench
RA	Regulations for the Army
RAT	Report on Application for Trial
RC	Regimental Commission
RCA	Riot Control Agent
RCM	Rules for Courts Martial
RFI	Request for Informations
RFP	Request for Proposal
RMSI	Regional Maritime Security Initiative

ROE	Rules of Engagement
ROI	Record Office Instructions
RP	Risk Purchase
RPC	Ranbir Penal Code
RT	Report on Trial
RVC	Remount & Veterinary Corps
SACEUR	Supreme Allied Commander in Europe
SAR	Search and Rescue Operation
SB	Selection Board
SC	Security Council
SCAP	Services Capital Acquisition Plan
SCI	Sensitive Compartmented Information
SCM	Summary Court-Martial
SCU	Serious Crimes Unit
SEPC	Staff Equipment Policy Committee
SG	Secretary General
SGCM	Summary General Court-Martial
SHQ	Service Headquarters
SJA	Staff Judge Advocate
SKD	Semi Knocked Down
SME	Subject Matter Expert
SO	Supply Order
SOC	Statement of Case
SOE	Summary of Evidence
SOF	Special Operations Forces
SOLAS	Safety of Life at Sea Convention
SPCM	Special Court-Martial
SQR	Services Qualitative Requirements
SRDS	Stock Return and Demand Statement
SRE	Security Related Expenditure
SS	Short Service
SSCO	Short Service Commission Officer
SSCRA	Soldiers' and Sailors' Civil Relief Act (USA)

SUA	Suppression of Unlawful Acts
TA	Territorial Army
TCN	Third Country National
TE	Tender Enquiry
TEC	Tender Evaluation Committee
TIP	Trafficing in Persons
TNCO	Trans National Criminal Organisations
TOC	Technical Oversight Committee
TOT	Transfer of Technology
TS	Time Scale/Territorial Sea
TSC	Technical Standardisation Committee
TT	Transnational Threat
UAVs	Unmanned Aerial Vehicles
UCAV	Unmanned Combat Aerial Vehicle
UCMJ	Uniform Code of Military Justice
UNCAT	UN Convention against Torture and Other Cruel, Inhuman or Degrading Treatment or Punishment
UNCLOS	United Nations Convention on Law of the Sea
UNDC	United Nations Office on Drugs & Crime
UNHCR	UN High Commission for Refugees
UNJLC	UN Joint Logistics Centre
UNSC	UN Security Council
UNWCC	United National War Crimes Commission
VCAS	Vice Chief of Air Staff
VCNS	Vice Chief of Naval Staff
VCOAS	Vice Chief of the Army Staff
VIC	Virtual Information Centre
WCR	War Crimes Report
WCS	Weapons Control Status
WMD	Weapons of Mass Destruction
WO	Warrant Officer
WSES	Women Special Entry Scheme
XO	Executive Officer

GLOSSARY OF MILITARY LEGAL TERMS

A

Abandoned Explosive Ordnance

Explosive ordnance that has not been used during an armed conflict, that has been left behind or dumped by a party to an armed conflict, and which is no longer under control of the party that left it behind or dumped it. Abandoned explosive ordnance may or may not have been primed, fused, armed or otherwise prepared for use. *See* Article 2.3 of Protocol on Explosive Remnants of War (Protocol V to the 1980 Convention).

Abandoned or Lost Property

Personal or movable property found on the defence establishment and appearing to have been abandoned or lost by its owner or the person entitled to the property.

See Canada National Defence Act, C. 35, section 44(1).

Abetment

A person may make himself responsible for the crime of another by instigating, conspiring with, or intentionally aiding the actual criminal in one of the ways described in the IPC (sections 107 and 108). In such cases, he cannot be charged with the actual offence committed by the other, and must be charged with "abetting" that offence. *See* Army Act, sections 66 to 69.

Abnormal

Different from what is usual or expected; [RA(DSR), para 601].

Abort

To terminate a mission for any reason other than enemy action. It may occur at any point after the beginning of the mission and prior to its completion.

Abrogate

To put an end to, to set aside, to revoke. To abolish by official, authoritative or formal action, to annul a formal law by an act of legislative power. A law is abrogated when it is totally annulled. *See* Article 33 of the Constitution.

Abscond

To hide, to depart clandestinely, to conceal oneself to avoid legal process.

Absconder

One who absconds; one who hides to escape a legal process.

Absconding

To hide. A person may hide even in his place of residence or away from it and in either case he will be absconding when he does so.

Absence

Non appearance, opposed to presence, the state of being away.

Absence Without Leave

A military offence punishable under the Military law which refers to voluntary absence from duty. A person is said to be absent without leave when he is voluntarily absent *i.e.*, absent due to circumstances within his control, without authority, from the place he knows, or ought to know, his duty requires him to be.

Absolute

Complete, perfect, final; absolute majority is one comprising more than half of the total number of votes.

Absolute Right

Right which can be exercised against everyone.

Abuse of Rights

Doctrine according to which an unmotivated or unreasonable exercise of a right amounts to an illegal act.

Access

Approach or the means or power of approaching.

Accessory

When a person is responsible for an offence by way of rendering assistance or common intent, he is equally responsible and liable to the same punishment as the principal offender; he may be tried before the principal offender has been tried and may be convicted even if the principal offender has been acquitted. Such a person if not present, either actually or constructively, at the actual commission of the offence is called an accessory before the fact, if the offence is a felony.

Accident

Denotes some unexpected event happening, though there may be negligence on the part of the person meeting with an accident. It would include not only such obvious occurrences as collisions, tripping over floor obstacles, fall of roof but also less obvious ones causing injury such as strain which causes capture, exposure to a draught causing chill, exertion causing apoplexy and shock causing neurasthenia. It would also include a heart attack which is an unexpected event happening without design. See *State of Punjab* v. *Kamlesh Devi*, Mil LJ 2004 P&H 67.

Accompanying

One may be "accompanying" an armed force though not directly employed by the military, *e.g.*, an individual moving with a military operation or has activities dependent upon and not merely incidental to the armed forces activities. *See* Army Act, section 2(1)(i). A civilian may no longer serve with military but may continue to remain closely affiliated with a military community.

Accompanying has been interpreted broader than "serving with".

Accomplice

An accomplice is a guilty associate or a guilty partner in crime. He is a competent witness against an accused, and a conviction may be based upon his uncorroborated testimony. *See* IEA, section 133.

Accountability

The obligation imposed by lawful order or regulation of an officer or other person for keeping accurate record of property, documents or funds. The person having this obligation may or may not have actual possession of the property, document, or funds. Accountability is concerned primarily with records, while responsibility is concerned primarily with custody, care and safe keeping.

Accoutrements

In a military sense signify habits, equipments, or furniture of a soldier such as buffs, belts, pouches, cartridge boxes etc.

Accuracy

Precision, correctness.

Accusation

The charging of a person with crime. *See* Army Act, section 56(a).

Accused

A person against whom an allegation has been made that he has committed an offence, or who is charged with an offence.

Accuser

Any person who signs and swears to charges, any person who directs that charges be signed and sworn to by another.

Acquiescence

Tacit consent which may be inferred from silence when, in good faith, no other interpretation is possible.

Acquittal

The word acquittal is by the judgment of a court and means that the person concerned has been clearly and fully exonerated of the charges levelled against him.

Acquittance Roll

A roll containing the names of the men of each troop or company or regiment, showing the debts and credits, with the signature of each man, and certificate of the officer commanding it.

Act

Statutes or Acts of Parliament.

Act of Hostility

Any act related to the conflict, which prejudices or may prejudice the physical integrity of protected objects.

Acting Rank

The rank provisionally held by a non-commissioned officer or higher official which may later be changed to the substantive rank.

Activation

Call up for full time military duty.

Active Duty

In relation to a person subject to the National Security Guard Act, 1986, means any duty as a member of the Security Guard during the period in which such person is attached to, or forms part of, a unit of Security Guard—

(i) which is engaged in operations against terrorists or any person in arms against the Union; or

(ii) which is operating at a picket or engaged on patrol or any other duty, in relation to combating terrorist activity.

See section 2(1)(a) of the NSG Act, 1986.

Active List

The expression includes officers on full or half pay; but does not include retired officers, recalled to service or re employed.

Active Service

The time during which a person subject to military law – (a) is attached to, or forms part of, a force which is engaged in operations against an enemy, or (b) is engaged in military operations, in or is on the line of march to, a country or place, wholly or partly occupied by an enemy, or (c) is attached to or forms part of a force which is in military occupation of a foreign country. *See* Army Act, section 3(i). Central Government may, by notification, declare certain persons on active service. *See* Army Act, section 9 and Navy Act, section 3(1).

Acts of War

Include unarmed combat, intelligence gathering and many other activities that do not cause damage to personnel or equipment.

Actual knowledge

The doctrine postulates that the war crime must be directly traceable to the superior, or his failure to supervise subordinates must constitute criminal negligence before criminal responsibility is imposed.

Adaptation

It carries with it the idea of modification for new uses or change in form or structure. *See* Army Act, section 2(1)(e).

Adequately Exercised Tenure

This is the minimum mandatory tenure for which an officer must earn reports in criteria or part criteria appointments before he can be awarded a definite grading by the selection board.

Adhoc

For a particular purpose.

Adhoc Tribunals

Two International Criminal Tribunals set up by the United Nations Security Council, acting under Chapter VII of the United Nations Charter to punish crimes committed in relation to two specific contexts: the former Yugoslavia and Rwanda.

Additional

Added, existing in addition.

Additional Protocols

These protocols are intended to supplement the Conventions by developing the protection of civilians in time of war and extending the criteria for the application of humanitarian law to cover new types of conflict. Protocol I applicable in international armed conflicts, including wars of national liberation, ensures the protection of civilians against the effect of hostilities, particularly bombardment. Protocol II supplements Article 3 common to all four Geneva Conventions, with more detailed rules applicable in situations which are not covered by Protocol I *i.e.,* internal armed conflicts of a certain magnitude.

Addresses

A formal speech or written statement made at a court-martial on behalf of or against the accused.

Adduce

To bring forward, advance, cite.

Adjournment

A putting-off until another time or transferring to a different place. The term refers only to an inquiry or court-martial trial which is already convened and which is thereafter postponed.

Adjutant

A regimental staff officer whose duties are to assist the Commanding Officer in the training, administration and maintenance of discipline in the unit. *See* RA(DSR), para 41.

Adjutant General

An officer of distinction selected to assist the General of an Army in all his operations. The duties of the Adjutant General relate to the discipline and general efficiency of the Army.

Administer

To furnish, to give, to dispense, to tender.

Administration

The management and execution of all military matters not included in tactics, operations and strategy; primarily in the fields of logistics and personnel management. It includes internal management of units.

Administrative Action

It is corrective action taken against a service personnel with regard to a lapse or fault noticed.

Administrative Control

Direction or exercise of authority over subordinate or other organisations in respect of administrative matters such as personnel management, supply, services, and other matters not included in the operational missions of the subordinate or other organisations.

Administrative Corrective Measures

The measures which a commanding officer or officer-in-charge is authorised to use by way of non-punitive disciplinary action to further the efficiency of his command or unit, when faced with minor violations of the military code or other deficiencies. These could be in the nature of withholding pass privileges, commissary privileges, on-post driving privileges, housing privileges, admonition, corrective training etc.

Administrative Restraint

Limitations on a service member imposed for operational or other military purposes independent of military justice, including administrative hold for medical reasons. *Ref.* UCMJ, Rules for Court-Martial, 304(h).

Admissible

Proper to be received, capable and worthy of being admitted. As applied to evidence, the term means that it is of such a character that the court or judge is bound to receive it, that is allow it to be introduced in evidence.

Admission

It is a statement made by a party to the proceedings, or his representative as to the subject matter of the case, or the relevant facts thereto. *See* IEA, sections 17 to 22. It is a self-incriminatory statement falling short of a complete acknowledgment of guilt.

Admonishment

It is an administrative action for first offences which are not of an aggravated nature. *See* RA(DSR), para 325.

Admonition

Mild, kind yet earnest reproof; cautionary advice or warning.

Advantage

Interest, increase, any office or dignity and forbearance to demand any money or money's worth or valuable thing.

Adversary

A party acknowledged as potentially hostile to a friendly party and against which the use of force may be envisaged.

Adverse

Negative, unpleasant, not likely to produce a good result. *See* Army Rule 14.

Adviser

One who gives advice or counsel, one designated to give advice.

Affairs of State

These include all maters of a public nature with which the Government is concerned. *See* Note 1 to Army Act, section 136.

Affection

Kind feeling, tender attachment.

Affirmation

A solemn declaration without taking oath.

Affray

It is committed when two or more persons fight in a public place and disturb public peace. *See* Note 1 to Army Act, section 42 read with IPC, section 159.

Afresh

Again, especially from the beginning or with new ideas.

Agenda

A list of items to be discussed at a meeting.

Agent

A person employed to do any act for another. A person acting on behalf of a hostile agency to promote its interest. In the intelligence field a person authorised or instructed to obtain or to assist in obtaining information for intelligence or counter-intelligence purposes. In intelligence usage, one who is recruited, trained, controlled and employed to obtain and report information.

Agreement

A coming together of parties in opinion or final determination; a mutual assent to do a thing, the union of two or more minds in a thing done or to be done.

Aggression

Resort to force contrary to international obligations.

Aid to Civil Authorities

A term used when troops are called to perform any of the following duties—(i) maintenance of law and order, (ii) maintenance of essential services, (iii) assistance during natural calamities such as earthquakes and floods, (iv) any other type of assistance which may be needed by the civil authorities. *See* RA(DSR), para 301.

Air

Air or airspace means the air up to an altitude of approximately 100 kilometers above mean sea level.

See HPCR Draft Manual on Air and Missile Warfare.

Air Force

Officers and airmen who by their commission, warrant, terms of enrolment or otherwise, are liable to render continuously for a term air force service to the Union in every part of the world, including persons belonging to any Air Force Reserve or the Auxiliary Air Force when called out on permanent service. *See* section 3(iv) of the Air Force Act.

Air Force Law

The law enacted by the Air Force Act and the rules made thereunder and includes the usages of the service. *See* section 3(vi), Air Force Act.

Air & Missile Warfare

Air and missile operations mean military operations involving either air to air, air to ground or ground to air; air to sea or sea to air, whether in offence or defence; and whether or not over the territory of one of the belligerent parties.

See HPCR Draft Manual on Air and Missile Warfare.

Aircraft

Any vehicle that can fly and carry goods or passengers. Vide section 3(ii) of the Air Force Act, it includes aeroplanes, balloons, kite balloons, airships, gliders or other machines for flying. It also means flying machines and guided missiles that derive their lift in flight chiefly from aerodynamic forces, and flying devices that are supported chiefly by their buoyancy in air and includes any aeroplane, balloon, kite balloon, airship, glider or kite. Section 2(1) of the National Defence Act, 1985, Canada, gives its meaning as any vehicle that can derive support in the atmosphere from the reaction of the air. There are five categories of aircraft: military, auxiliary, state, civil and medical.

* Military aircraft means any aircraft other than medical aircraft – under command by members of the armed forces of a belligerent party and marked as such.

* Auxiliary aircraft means any aircraft other than military or medical aircraft – owned by or under the exclusive control of a belligerent party.

* State aircraft means any aircraft owned or used by a belligerent party, serving exclusively State functions. Such aircraft include military aircraft and auxiliary aircraft, as well as aircraft used for public service such as police and customs or other Governmental functions.

* Civil aircraft means any aircraft other than military, auxiliary or State aircraft.

* Medical aircraft means any aircraft under the control of a belligerent party, whether military or civilian, permanently or temporarily assigned exclusively to aerial transportation of wounded, sick or shipwrecked persons, and/or the transport of medical personnel and equipment.

See HPCR Draft Manual on Air and Missile Warfare.

Aircraft Material

Includes any engines, fittings, guns, gear, instruments or apparatus for use in connection with aircraft, and any of its components and accessories and petrol oil, and any other substance used for providing motive power for planes. *See* Air Force Act, section 3(iii).

Airman

An enlisted man in the air force.

Alarm

An alarm among soldiers in the Army is not so much a danger as a warning against danger; an alarm, signified by firing of a gun or a beating of a drum, denotes to an army or camp that the enemy is suspected of intending a sudden surprise or that the surprise has actually been made.

Alert

(a) To forewarn, to prepare for action, defence or protection.

(b) A warning signal of a real or threatened danger such as an air attack.

(c) The period of time during which troops standby in response to an alarm.

Alibi

When an accused is charged with an offence alleged to have been committed at a particular place and at or within a specified time, and the defence evidence points to his presence elsewhere at that particular time so as to be inconsistent with his presence as alleged, the excuse is known as an alibi.

All Ranks

Officers, Junior Commissioned Officers and Other Ranks who are in service in the Army.

Allegiance

The obligation of fidelity which the individual owes to the Government or to the Sovereign under which he lives in return for the protection he receives.

Alliance

In a military sense signifies a treaty entered into by sovereign States, for their mutual safety and defence. It is a permanent collective defence relationship among two or more States provided for in an international agreement. Also defined as the result of formal agreements between two or more nations for broad, long term objectives that further the common interests of the participating members.

Allotment

Determination and intimation of a specific building, plot, dwelling unit, servant quarter, car parking space or car garage, scooter parking space or scooter garage aginst booking of a registrant. *See* AWHO Master Brochure, July 1987.

Ally

A nation fighting or pledged to fight on the side of another.

Alteration

To make different. Alteration of finding or sentence is provided for when a finding is found for any reason to be invalid or cannot be supported by evidence. *See* Army Act, section 163.

Alternative

The one or the other of two things, a privilege of choosing one of two things or courses.

Alternative Charge

These are framed when doubt exists as to which offence has been committed. The most serious charge should be placed first. *See* Note 2 to Army Act, section 139 and Note 6 to Army Rule 28.

Alternative Dispositions

Military offences may be dealt with through non-punitive measures, non-judicial punishment and an array of judicial alternatives. These are sanctions for the enforcement of military code in the area of minor offences.

Amenable

Easy to control, willing to be influenced by.

Amend

To correct, rectify or reform. All these words convey the idea of making a thing better or bringing things into a more perfect state.

Ammunition

The complete round or its component including cartridge cases, primers, propellant power, bullets or projectiles, that are used in a fire-arm, provided those components are themselves subject to authorisation by the respective State Party. [Article 3(e) of Protocol against the Illicit Manufacturing and Trafficking in Fire-arms, their Parts and Components and Ammunition, supplementing the United Nations Convention against Transnational Organised Crime.]

Amnesty

An act of oblivion, or forgiveness of past offences committed against the State. The effect of the act is, that crimes so obliterated cannot again be brought up against the guilty parties. Usually an act of amnesty is meant to include a number of individuals guilty of offences of a political nature, as rebellion etc.

Analogy

Process of reasoning from similar cases or situations.

Animal

The word denotes any living creature, other than a human being. *See* section 47, the Indian Penal Code.

Annex

A supplement to an order or other communication which supplies details or a clarification of the order or communication. *See* Army Rule 54(3).

Announce

To make public or give official intimation of.

Annual Acquisition Plan

The annual requirement of funds for capital acquisitions taking into account the schemes listed in five years services capital acquisition plan and those proposed for the year ahead, carryovers, operational exigencies and proposed changes in priorities.

Annuity

A yearly payment of a certain sum of money, granted to another for life or for years, and chargeable only on the person of the grantor.

Annul

To make void, to destroy, to cancel, do away with.

Annulment

The act of annulling, the act of making void retrospectively as well as prospectively. *See* RA(DSR), para 708(a)(i).

Ante-Date

Pre date. *See* Army Rule 2(d)(iii).

Anti Handling Devices

A device intended to protect a mine and which is part of, linked to, attached to or placed under the mine and which activates when an attempt is made to tamper with the Mine. *See* Article 2 of the Protocol on Prohibitions or Restrictions on the Use of Mines, Booby Traps and Other Devices as Amended on 3 May, 1996.

Anti Personnel Mine

A mine primarily designed to be exploded by the presence, proximity or contact of a person and that will incapacitate, injure or kill one or more persons. *See* Article 2 of the Protocol on Prohibitions or Restrictions on the Use of Mines, Booby-Traps and Other Devices as amended on 3 May, 1996.

Anticipatory Pension

If a retiring pension has been earned and there is likely to be delay in sanction, the Controller of Defence Accounts (Pension) had the power to issue anticipatory pension upon a laid down declaration made by the pensioner. This term is now not used commonly.

Anticipatory Self Defence

Justifying use of force to repel not just actual armed attacks, but also 'imminent' armed attacks.

Anti Terrorism

Anti terrorism covers all preventive measures taken to reduce the probability of a terrorist act occurring, *i.e.*, prevent, deter and respond to terrorism. The measures could include continuous evaluation of national policy related to terrorism, continuous assessment of all major threats and creation of standard emergency response protocols for all potential terrorist threats and actions, besides other measures.

Apartheid

The crime of apartheid means inhuman acts of a character similar to those of crimes against humanity, committed in the context of an institutionalised regime of systematic oppression and domination by one racial group over any other racial group or groups and committed with the intention of maintaining that regime. *See* Article 2.1(h) of the ICC Statute.

Appeal

A challenge.

Appearance

The action of appearing formally, the coming into a court as a party, effective appearance.

Appellate Review

The after-review of the record of trial by a Judge Advocate and action by the convening authority under UCMJ.

Appendix

An addition sub-jointed to a document or book having some contributory value but not essential to completeness.

Appertain

To belong or refer to somebody/something; RA(DSR), para 827.

Appoint

To choose somebody for a job or position of responsibility. *See* Army Rule 151.

Appointing Authority

With reference to a military court or board, etc., the officer who selects and appoints its member.

Apprehend

Implies the seizing or confining of any person; as to apprehend a deserter etc.

Apprehension

It is the military counterpart to civilian arrest, for it involves, "the taking of a person into custody". Apprehension involves restraint on the accused's personal freedom until he is handed over to the proper authorities; thus it goes beyond arrest by imposing physical restraint.

Apprehension Roll

Is the report issued by the Commanding Officer of a unit in the event of desertion or absence without leave of a person subject to the Army Act. It is sent to the authorities listed in RA(DSR), para 377.

Appropriate

To make a thing one's own, to set apart for, or assign for a particular use to the exclusion of all other use.

Appropriation

The assignment to meet specified expenditure of funds at the disposal of the assigning authority. *See* Financial Regulations, Part I, section 1. In the context of element of War Crimes under the Rome Statute, the term means to take, obtain or withhold property, theft, requisition, spoliation. A definite transfer of title as to the property seized or exploited is not necessary.

Approval

The act of accepting as satisfactory, the action of approving, to accept as good or sufficient for the purpose intended, to pronounce good.

Arbitration

(1) In its wider sense: binding settlement of a dispute by a third party. (2) In its narrower sense: settlement on a legal basis by a third party.

Area Command

A command which is composed of those organised elements of one or more of the armed services, designed to operate in a specific geographical area, which are placed under a single commander.

Area Commander (*See* Officer Commanding the Area).

Area of Responsibility

Area of responsibility is the spatial extent over which a commander must exercise control. It will be expressed in terms of frontage and depth and, as far as possible, have clearly identifiable flank and rear boundaries.

Area Target

A target consisting of an area rather than a single point.

Armament

Weapons with a lethal capability.

Armed Conflict

The term suggests the existence of hostilities between armed forces organised to a greater or lesser extent. It is use of armed force by one State against the territory of another. It may also be in the form of a confrontation between the Government and a rebel movement. An international armed conflict may begin in any one of three ways:

(i) by declaration of war;

(ii) by the announcement of one State that it considers itself to be at war with another State; or

(iii) through the commission of hostile acts employing military forces by one state against another.

It may be terminated by:

(a) a treaty of peace;

(b) a cessation of hostilities and establishment of peaceful relations without a treaty;

(c) unconditional surrender; or

(d) subjugation.

It is also defined as a situation in which violence or military force is threatened or used. Generally it is a contest between two opposing sides, each seeking to impose its will on the other; however intra-state conflict may involve several factions.

Armed Conflict Not of an International Character

The ICTR refers to the following non-cumulative, and therefore, alternative reference criteria—

1. That the party in revolt against the *de jure* Government possesses an organised military force, an authority responsible for its acts, acting within a determinate territory and having the means of respecting and ensuring the respect for the convention.
2. That the legal Government is obliged to have recourse to the regular military forces against insurgents organised as military, in possession of a part of the national territory.
3. (a) That the *de jure* Government has recognised the insurgents as belligerents; or

   (b) That it has claimed for itself the rights of a belligerent; or

   (c) That it has accorded the insurgents recognition as belligerents for the purposes only of the present convention; or

   (d) That the dispute has been admitted to the agenda of the Security Council or the General Assembly of the United Nations as being a threat to international peace, a breach of peace, or an act of aggression.

Armed Forces

The armed forces of a party to a conflict consists of all organised armed forces, groups and units which are under a command responsible to that party for the conduct of its subordinates. *See* Article 43, para I of AP I. For the purposes of the Armed Forces (Special Powers) Act, 1958, the term means the military forces and the air forces operating as land forces, and includes other armed forces of the Union so operating. These include ground, naval and air forces of a nation.

Under the Hague Rules 2, the term 'armed forces' are comprises—

(i) The army: this includes militia or volunteers corps in countries where they constitute the national forces or form part of them. The members of the army are entitled to recognition as belligerent forces whether they have joined voluntarily or have been compelled to do so by State law, whether they are nationals of the enemy or of a neutral State, and whether they joined before or after the declaration of war.

(ii) Militia or volunteer corps which do not ordinarily form part of the army, but have been raised possibly for the duration of the war or even for the execution of some special operation. These irregular troops must, however, fulfil all of the following conditions—

(a) Be commanded by a person responsible for his subordinates;

(b) Have a fixed distinctive sign recognizable at a distance;

(c) Carry arms openly; and

(d) Conduct their operations in accordance with the laws and customs of war.

(iii) The inhabitants of a territory not under occupation who, on the approach of an enemy, spontaneously take up arms to resist the invading troops without having had time to organise themselves as laid down in (i) or (ii), provided they conform to conditions (c) and (d) laid down above for irregular combatants.

Armed Insurrection

The action of raising in arms or open resistance (with arms) against established authority or Governmental restraint.

Armed Neutrality

The maintenance by a nation of an armed force held ready to repel any aggression on the part of belligerent nations between which it is neutral.

Armistice

A truce, or suspension of hostilities, between two armies or two nations by mutual agreement.

Arms Control Agreement

The written or unwritten embodiment of the acceptance of one or more arms control measures by two or more nations.

Army

The Army is composed of those who have undertaken a definite liability for military service; *viz*, combatant troops, administrative service/departments and enrolled non-combatants. It comprises – the regular Army, the Army Reserve and the Territorial Army. *See* RA(DSR), para 1.

In certain nations 'army' is the land component of the armed forces.

Army Corps

A formation larger than a division but smaller than an army, or army group. It usually consists of two or more divisions together with supporting arms and services. *See* Army Rule 202.

Army List

A publication issued by the defence department. It contains the names of all commissioned officers of the army including the civil departments, enumerated alphabetically and by regiment.

Army Number

Fixed numbers allotted by the Officer-in-Charge Records concerned to all personnel enrolled into the Army as well as civilians with a field service liability. *See* RA(DSR), para 624.

Army Regulations

Government directives for the operation of the Army. The Army Regulations constitute the basic rules and policies along which the army operates.

Arraignment

It consists of calling upon the accused by his number, rank, name and description, as given in the charge-sheet and asking him 'Is that your number, rank, name and unit or description?', reading all charges to him and asking him to plead guilty or not guilty to each charge separately. *See* Army Rule 48 and notes thereto. The Judge Advocate (if any) or, in his absence the presiding officer, conducts the arraignment.

Arrest

A restraint of a man's person obliging him to be obedient to the law. It is said to be done when one is taken and restrained from his liberty. Arrest is either close arrest or open arrest. When arrest is not described by the authority ordering it as open arrest, it means close arrest. *See* RA(DSR), para 392. It means the act of apprehending a person for the alleged commission of an offence or by the action of an authority. Moral restraint imposed on a person by oral or written orders of the competent authority limiting the person's personal liberty pending disposition of the charges.

Arrest in Quarters

Restriction of a person to the room, building or other place where he lives, while awaiting trial by court-martial or other judicial or disciplinary action, usually applied to commanding officers. It is moral restraint limiting an officer's liberty, imposed as a non-judicial punishment by a flag or general officer-in-command.

Arson

It is one of the instances of malicious injury and consists in unlawfully and maliciously setting fire to buildings or to certain peculiarly inflammable kinds of property.

Article 15

An article of the Uniform Code of Military Justice providing a procedure for investigating and punishing minor misconduct by military members.

Article 39a Session

A session of a court-martial called by the military judge either before the members are seated or after that phase of the trial has begun under UCMJ.

Articles of War

These were made by the Crown for the governance of its troops. They provided a common code for the officers and soldiers. They could be altered and enlarged at the pleasure of the King. And in certain cases extended to civilians – as when by proclamation any place shall be put under martial law; or when the people follow a camp or army for the sake of merchandise, or serve in any menial capacity. It was ordained, that the articles of war shall be read in the circle of each regiment belonging to the British Army every month, or oftener, if the commanding officer thought proper. A recruit or soldier was not liable to be tried by a military tribunal; unless it could be proved that the articles of war had been duly read to him.

Ascertain

To find out the true or correct information.

Assault

Whoever makes any gesture or any preparation, intending or knowing it to be likely that such a gesture or preparation will cause any person present to apprehend that he who makes that gesture or preparation is about to use criminal force to that person, is said to commit assault. *See* IPC, section 351.

Assemble

To come together as a group, to fit together all the separate parts of something. *See* Army Rule 27(3).

Assent

Official agreement to or approval of something, to agree to a request, an idea or a suggestion. *See* Army Rule 148.

Assessed

A judgment made about the nature or quality of somebody or something. *See* Army Act, section 89(2).

Assessment

An assessment of the mental condition of the accused person and any incidental observation or examination of the accused person. Section 197 of Canada's National Defence Act, 1985.

Assign

To grant, to convey, to point out, to transfer or make over to another the right one has in any object. *See* Army Act, section 69.

Associated Personnel

Means—

(i) Persons assigned by a Government or an inter-Governmental organisation with the agreement of the competent organ of the United Nations;

(ii) Persons engaged by the Secretary-General of the United Nations or by a specialised agency or by the International Atomic Energy Agency;

(iii) Persons deployed by a humanitarian non-Governmental organisation or agency under an agreement with the Secretary-General of the United Nations or with a specialized agency or with the International Atomic Energy Agency;

to carry out activities in support of the fulfillment of the mandate of the United Nations operations.

[1994 Convention on the Safety of United Nations and Associated Personnel.]

Association

A body of persons acting together, upon the methods and forms used by incorporated bodies for the prosecution of some common enterprise. *See* Army Act, section 21.

Asylum Seeker

A person who invokes the protection of the 1951 United Nations Convention relating to the Status of Refugees before the national authorities of a State and claims persecution to gain official refugee status in that country.

Asymmetric Warfare

Situations where due to the availability of high technology weapons in the hands of one of the parties to an armed conflict, there is a clear imbalance between the belligerents.

Attach

The placement of units or personnel in an organisation where such placement is relatively temporary. Subject to limitations imposed in the attachment order, the commander of the formation, unit or organisation receiving the attachment will exercise the same degree of command control thereover as he does over the units and persons organic to his command. However, the responsibility for transfer and promotion of personnel will normally be retained by the parent formation.

Attached

An individual or unit is said to be attached when placed temporarily under the direct orders of the commander of a unit other than the one of which such individual or unit forms an organic component.

Attached To

Within the meaning of the Territorial Army Act, the term is used in relation to the liability of an enrolled person to perform military service with any regular forces either at his own request or under the prescribed conditions. *See* section 7(3)(c) of the TA Act, 1948.

Attachment

Moving a man temporarily from his Corps and attaching him for pay, rations, quarters, discipline, or any of them, to another unit without in any way affecting his status in his own Corps; this can be done without his consent.

Attacks

The term means acts of violence against the adversary, whether in offence or in defence. *See* AP I, Article 49(1).

Attain

To succeed in getting something, usually after a lot of effort. *See* Army Rule 16A.

Attempt to Desert

Some act which, if completed, would constitute desertion, *e.g.* one arrested in the act of leaving his unit lines without authority dressed in plain clothes and carrying his personal kits.

Attestation

It is administration to the enrolled person of the oath or affirmation of military fidelity. *See* Army Act, sections 16 and 17 and Army Rule 8. All those who are enrolled as combatants, those selected to hold NCO or acting NCO ranks, and other persons as prescribed by the Central Government are to be attested.

Audit

To draw up or present an account. *See* RA(DSR), para 834. The systematic examination of records and documents to determine:

* The adequacy and effectiveness of budgeting, accounting, finance and related policies and procedures;
* Compliance with applicable statutes, regulations, policies, and prescribed procedures;
* The reliability, accuracy, and completeness of financial and administrative records and reports; and
* The extent to which funds and other resources are properly protected and effectively used.

Ref. Glossary of selected Terms: The Management of Security Assistance.

Authenticate

To give legal validity to, to establish the genuineness of. *See* Army Rule 63.

Authorisation to Search

It is an express permission, written or oral, issued by competent military authority to search a person or an area for specified property or evidence or for a specific person and to seize such property, evidence or person. It may contain an order directing subordinate personnel to conduct a search in a specified manner. [US MRE 315(b)(1).]

Authorised Follower

Persons other than officers, soldiers or airmen, who are employed by, or are in the service of, the Forces or Corps concerned, or are in the service of any officer, soldier or airman of such forces or Corps. *See* section 2 of the Indian Tolls (Army and Air Force) Act, 1901.

Authorised Strength

The largest number of members authorised to be in an armed force, a component, a branch, a grade or any other category of the armed forces.

Authoritative Interpretation

Interpretation of a document by the parties in a subsequent document.

Authority

The legal power to act or issue commands or orders, to take action and measures; and to enforce obedience, a right to command, and a consequence right to be obeyed; an individual or organisation that exercises or may exercise such power.

Auto Interpretation

Determination by an interested party of its own legal duties.

Autopsy

An official examination of dead body by a doctor in order to discover the cause of death.

Auxiliary

Foreign or subsidiary troops which were furnished to a belligerent power in consequence of a treaty alliance, or for pecuniary considerations.

Auxiliary Service

The militia, yeomanry, and volunteers form what are termed the auxiliary forces; a soldier serving with another nation.

Averment

Act of averring, that which is averred, affirmation, positive assertion, a positive statement of facts.

Award

The sentence or determination of a military court.

B

Bad Conduct Discharge

One of two types of punitive discharges that may be imposed on an enlisted person under UCMJ.

Badge

A distinguished mark or medal worn on the colours of a regiment; insignia denoting special skill or experiences used mainly for identification.

Bailee

A person is a bailee of an article when it is delivered to him for the purpose of ultimately redelivering it, or delivering it to some other person.

Ban

A proclamation made sometimes to prevent the men from quitting camp, at others to enforce the rigour of military discipline.

Barracks

Means permanent structures for the accommodation of soldiers, as distinguished from huts and tents which have a square or open place in front for the purpose of drill and parade.

Barrack Damage

Damage to or loss or destruction of any premises in which soldiers are quartered or billeted, or any appurtenances, fixtures, furniture or effects therein or appertaining thereto.

Basic Pay

Pay in the pay scale of the rank including stagnation increment, if any. Basic Pay does not include Flying Allowance, Qualification Allowance, Technical Pay, Personal Pay or any other type of Special Pay. *See* Special Army Instructions 2/S/1998.

Batch

A batch comprises of all officers reckoning seniority within a particular calendar year.

Battery

A battery consists of two or more pieces of artillery in the field. It is an assault in which the attempt or offer to do bodily harm is consummated by the infliction of that harm.

Battle

It is a state of combat between major forces, each having opposing (assigned or perceived) operational missions. Each side seeks to impose its will on the opponent by accomplishing its mission, while preventing the opponent from achieving his. A battle starts when one side initiates combat, and ends when either side accomplishes its mission or when either or both fail to accomplish their missions. Battles are part of campaigns and normally last a few days or weeks.

Battle Casualties

Those sustained in action against enemy forces or whilst repelling enemy air attacks as per the detailed stipulations. Also defined as any casualty incurred as the direct result of hostile action sustained in combat or relating thereto or sustained while going to or returning from a combat mission.

Befitting

To be suitable and good enough for somebody/something. *See* Army Rule 76(1).

Before the Enemy

Whether a person is "before the enemy" is a question of tactical relation, not distance.

Beleagured

A person is beleagured, if he is a member of an organised element that has been surrounded by a hostile force to prevent escape of its members.

Belligerency

Is an armed conflict between sovereign States.

Belligerent Party

A party to an international armed conflict.

See HPCR Draft Manual on Air and Missile Warfare.

Bellum Justum

Just war.

Bench Trial

Based on a request by the accused, a trial where the military judge hears the evidence, determines guilt and imposes a sentence under UCMJ.

Besieged

A person is besieged, if he is a member of an organised element that has been surrounded by a hostile force for the purpose of compelling it to surrender.

Best Qualified

The term is used in relation to the people (by age, education, training, experience, length of service, and judicial temperament) available to the convening authority to select to serve as members of a court-martial.

Bestiality

Buggery with animals, including birds.

Bigamy

It is committed by a person who, being already married to one person, goes through the form of marriage with another person during the life of the former husband or wife.

Billet

A place, usually a private house, where a soldier is lodged.

Bind

To constrain, especially by legal authority. *See* RA(DSR), para 534.

Biological Weapons

These are:

(i) Microbial or other biological agents, or toxins whatever their origin or method of production, of types and in quantities that have no justification for prophylactic, protective or other peaceful purposes; and

(ii) Weapons, equipment or delivery systems specially designed to use such agents or toxins for hostile purposes or in armed conflict.

See section 4(a) of the Weapons of Mass Destruction and their Delivery Systems (Prohibition of Unlawful Activities) Act, 2005.

Bivouac

A night watch in open air. Troops bivouac when they make the best of it for the night, encamping in the open air.

Blockade

In international law, is the means in times of war of rendering intercourse with an enemy's port unlawful on the part of neutrals; and it is carried into effect by an armed force (ships of war), which blocks up and bars export or import to or from the place blockaded. A place is said to be blockaded when communication by water is cut off, and ingress and egress rendered dangerous by the presence of blockading warships.

Board of Inquiry

A board convened under the relevant service rules to investigate and report on the absence, death, capture or escape of any personnel, loss of or damage to service or public property, disablement of a ship or readiness for sea accident or any other matter referred to it by the convening authority.

Board of Officers

It is an assembly of officers convened for an object which should not involve any point of discipline. They will follow, as far as may be convenient, the rules for courts of inquiry, but are in no way bound by them. *See* RA(DSR), para 517. A number of officers assembled by military authority for the transaction of business.

Booby-trap

Any device or material which is designed, constructed or adapted to kill or injure and which functions unexpectedly when a person disturbs or approaches an apparently harmless object or performs an apparently safe act.

[Article 2(1) of Protocol on Prohibitions or Restrictions on the Use of Mines, Booby-Traps and Other Devices (Protocol II), Geneva, 10 October 1980.]

Booking Letter

A letter intimating the registrant that he has been booked for a dwelling unit in a particular scheme. Financial liabilities of the registrant commence with the issue of this letter. *See* AWHO Master Brochure, July 1987.

Border Out Post

Detachments of para military or police forces deployed along the international border for vigil and border management during peace time. Important border outposts are reorganised, reinforced by regular troops and may be re-sited during hostilities.

Breach of Peace

It is an unlawful breaking of the peace by an outward disturbance of a violent or turbulent nature.

Breaking Arrest

It is committed when the person in arrest infringes the limits set by orders. The reason for infringement is immaterial.

Brevet Rank

Specially meritorious service in peace or war performed by officers of the rank of captain, major and Lieutenant Colonel either at regimental duty or on staff, may be recognised by the grant of brevet promotion to the next higher rank. *See* RA(DSR), para 72.

Bribery

Is the corrupt giving or offering of any thing of value to a public official with the intent to:

(a) influence official acts;

(b) have the official perpetrate fraud or set up opportunity for fraud; or

(c) have that official do anything contrary to his public duty.

See 18 US Code, section 201.

Brief Reasons

After recording the finding on each charge, the court-martial shall give brief reasons in support thereof which are recorded in the proceedings. *See* Army Rule 62(1).

Brigade Area

One of the brigade areas, whether occupied by a brigade or not, into which India is for military purposes for the time being divided, and includes any area which the Governor General in Council may, by notification in the Gazette of India, declare to be a Brigade area for all or any of the purposes of this Act. *See* section 2(1)(a) of the Cantonment (House Accommodation) Act, 1923.

Brought in Transit

To bring goods from any country into India by land, air, or amphibious means of transportation, where the goods are to be taken out from India on the same conveyance on which they are brought into India without any landing in India; but does not include a conveyance in innocent passage through Indian territory, India territorial waters or Indian airspace of a foreign conveyance carrying goods.

Explanation I—A conveyance is a foreign conveyance if it is not registered in India.

Explanation II—A conveyance is in 'innocent passage' if it is not engaged in relevant activity and passes through or above Indian territorial waters or airspace without stopping or anchoring in India.

See section 4(b) of the Weapons of Mass Destruction and their Delivery Systems (Prohibition of Unlawful Activities) Act, 2005.

Buggery

Buggery with mankind consists of the penetration of the human anus, male or female, by the male genital organ, and it is complete upon proof of the slightest degree of penetration, whether there is an emission of seed or not.

Burden of Proof

The burden of proof for all elements of an offence (except lack of mental responsibility) is on the prosecution.

Burglary

Is the breaking and entering the dwelling house of another by night with intent to commit a felony therein.

Buy

Acquisitions covered under the outright purchase category.

Buy & Make

Capital acquisitions which are covered under the category of purchase followed by licensed production or indigenous development.

C

Cadet

This term is given to students who are being educated at a military college for the Army.

Calculated

Carefully planned to get what you want, a risk that you decide is worth taking even though you know it might have bad results. *See* Army Act, section 34(g).

Called Out

This term is used in relation to the liability of an enrolled person under the Territorial Army Act to act to perform military service in support of the civil power or to provide essential guards.

Called Upon

In relation to the Territorial Army provisions, this term is used in the context of service which a person is compulsorily liable to render.

Camp

The word includes a bivouac and any quarters, shelter or other place where troops are temporarily located. *See* Note 13 to Army Act, section 34.

Camp Follower

The settlers, petty tradesmen, servants and all other non-combatants who accompany any army in the field. All camp followers are subject to the articles of war, at whatever location.

Cancellation

The fact or an instance of cancelling; something that has been revoked or annulled or deleted. *See* RA(DSR), para 708(a)(i).

Cantonment

These are distinct situations, where the different parts of the Army lie as near to each other as possible, and in the same manner as they encamp in the field. Troops are considered to be in a cantonment for the purposes of the Army Act when they are quartered in any station or locality as a permanent, or semi permanent arrangement. *See* Note 6 to Army Act, section 64.

When troops are detached and quartered in different adjacent towns and villages, they are said to be placed in cantonments. The cantonments contain barracks and huts termed lines for the troops. The officers live for most part in bungalows or thatched houses. Regimental bazars also form part of the adjuncts of a cantonment.

Cantonment Authority

A Cantonment Board, or, in the case of a cantonment for which such a Board has not been constituted or has ceased to exist or cannot be convened, the officer commanding the station.

Cantonment Board

A Cantonment Board constituted under the Cantonment Act, 1924.

Capital Offence

An offence for which the maximum punishment includes the death penalty.

Capital Punishment

The sentence of death passed by a court-martial for certain offences committed by officers or men. Capital punishment is inflicted by the offender being either shot or hanged, the latter being resorted to for some scandalous or infamous crimes only.

Capitulation

It is an agreement between opposing commanders for the surrender of troops in a prescribed locality or district. It is not a contractual agreement and does not refer to the surrender of the entire state.

Capture

The act of taking or seizing by force, seizure, arrest, as to the capture of an enemy.

Captured

A person is captured if he or she has been seized as the result of action of an unfriendly military or paramilitary force in a foreign country.

Carriage

A vehicle for carriage, or haulage other than one specially constructed for use on rails.

Carries Away

In the context of theft, is the smallest amount of moving, so long as there is severance of the property from the possession of the person from whom it is taken, is sufficient.

Carnal Knowledge

Penetration is considered to constitute carnal knowledge.

Cashiering

The dismissal of an officer by a court-martial for dishonourable or disgraceful conduct; whereby he is rendered incapable of serving the Government for the future in any military capacity.

Cartel

In the wider sense of the term, it is used to signify a convention concluded between belligerents for the purpose of permitting certain kinds of non-hostile intercourse which would otherwise be prevented by the conditions of war. For instance, communication by post, trade in certain commodities, and such like, may be agreed upon by a cartel. As used in a strictly military sense, however, a cartel means an agreement for the exchange of prisoners of war.

Cartel Ship

It is a vessel engaged in the exchange of prisoners or in carrying official communications to the enemy. Such a ship is considered inviolable, but must not engage in any hostilities or carry any implements of war except a signal gun.

Casting Vote

Is the term used to denote the final and decisive vote which the law allows the Presiding Officer of a court-martial to give in case of an equality of votes.

Casts Away

To throw away, to allow to fall. *See* Army Act, section 34(c).

Casualty

Any person who is lost to his organisation, by reason of having been declared dead, interned, captured, retained, missing, missing in action, beleaguered, besieged or detained.

Casualty Return

A return submitted by the units and formations to higher authorities when a casualty takes place. All events in the career of an officer such as promotions, demotions, leave, admissions to and discharge from hospitals, transfers, absence, etc. which are to find a place in the record of service of an officer maintained by Army Headquarters shall be notified, as and when they occur in casualty returns.

Cause

Verb. To make something happen, especially something bad or unpleasant. *See* Army Act, section 37(a).

Causing Serious Injury to Body or Health

This offence entails the infliction of injury, which not necessarily causing death, will produce long-lasting and significant effects with respect to the victim's physical integrity or their physical or mental health.

Cause-Related Marketing

Relationships in which a company agrees to donate a specific amount of sales revenue (or an equivalent thereof) from a product, service, or brand, to a component of the Movement in return for the public association of its image with that of the Movement. *See* Annex to Resolution 10 of Substantive

Provision of the International Red Cross and Red Crescent Movement Policy for Corporate Sector Partnership.

Caution

The taking of heed, a precept or warning against evil of any kind. An explanation given previous to the word of command, by which soldiers are called to attend, that they may execute any given movement with unanimity and correctness. *See* Army Rule 77(3).

Caveat

A formal notice, or caution given by a party interested to a court, judge, or public officer, against performance of certain judicial or ministerial acts, a caution entered in a competent court, to stop probates, administrations, and such like, from being granted without the knowledge of the party that enters.

Censor

An official with the power to examine letters or correspondence.

Censure

An award made for a minor offence or a lapse to an officer or JCO. It may take the form of either 'displeasure' or 'severe displeasure' regarding which policy instructions are issued from time to time. It may either be of 'recordable' or 'non recordable' type.

Certificate

Written or printed statement which may be used as proof, made by somebody in authority.

Certifying

To confirm or attest, usually in writing, to endorse or guarantee that certain required standards have been met.

Cession

The transfer of territory by mutual agreement.

Chain of Command

The succession of commanding officers from a superior to a subordinate through which command is exercised, it is also called "Command channel".

Challenge

An opportunity provided to an accused at his trial by court-martial, other than summary court-martial, to oppose the detailment of an officer or more to serve at the court-martial as a member. In earlier times, the term applied to an objection made against any member of a court-martial, on the score of real or presumed partiality. The prisoner, however, in this case, must assign his cause of challenge. Also it is a warning by a sentry given to any person approaching his post after dark. It is formal objection to a member of the court or the military judge being allowed to continue to sit on a court-martial.

Character

The combination of traits and qualities distinguishing the individual nature of a person, moral force, reputation. *See* RA(DSR), para 517.

Charge

A charge means an accusation contained in a charge-sheet that a person subject to the Army Act has been guilty of an offence. It is the formal written charge upon which the accused is to be tried. *See* Army Rule 28. It comprises of statement of offence and particulars of the charge. *See* Army Rule 30(2). It is a written account of the offence. Every charge should state one offence only and in no case should an offence be described in the alternative in the same charge. A formal statement explaining the article of the Uniform Code of Military Justice which the accused is alleged to have violated.

Charge and Specification

A description in writing of the offence that the accused is alleged to have committed.

Charge Report

It is the duty of the person confining an accused to the commander of a guard or picquet, or the provost marshal, at the time of committal, or in any case within twenty-four hours, an account in writing, signed by himself, showing the offence with which the accused is charged. This report is called the 'charge' or the 'charge report'.

Charge Sheet

A document containing one or more charges. It is usually prepared by the CO or adjutant of the accused's unit. *See* Army Rule 28. There may be several charge sheets, but the court can only deal with one charge sheet at a time. When there are two or more charge sheets, they must be consecutively numbered.

Charged With

The expression means officially charged with, that is to say, in virtue of the public office which the accused formally holds.

Chemical Weapons

(i) The toxic chemicals and their precursors, except where intended for—

(a) Industrial, agricultural, research, medical, pharmaceutical or other peaceful purposes;

(b) Protective purposes, namely those purposes directly related to protection against toxic chemicals and to protection against chemical weapons;

(c) Military purposes not connected with the use of chemical weapons and not dependant on the use of toxic properties of chemicals as a method of warfare; or

(d) Law enforcement including domestic air control purposes, as long as the types and quantities are consistent with such purposes;

(ii) The munitions and devices, specially designed to cause death or other harm through the toxic properties of those toxic chemicals specified in sub clause (i) which would be released as a result of the employment of such munitions and devices; and

(iii) Any equipment specifically designed for use directly in connection with the employment of munitions and devices in sub clause (ii), together or separately.

See section 4(c) of the Weapons of Mass Destruction and Their Delivery Systems (Prohibition of Unlawful Activities) Act, 2005.

Chief Military Judge

Under Canada's National Defence Act, 1985, the Governor in Council may designate a military judge to be the Chief

Military Judge. The latter assigns military judges to preside at courts martial and to perform other judicial duties under the Act.

Chief of the Army Staff

Officer commanding the regular Army. *See* Army Act, section 3(iv). The Chief of the Army Staff is responsible to the President through the Central Government for the command, discipline, recruitment, training, organisation, administration and preparation for war of the Army. *See* RA(DSR), para 4.

Chief of the Naval Staff

Flag officer appointed by the President as Chief of the Naval Staff or in his absence on leave or otherwise an officer appointed by the Central Government to officiate as such or in the absence of such officiating appointment, the officer on whom the command devolves in accordance with regulations made under the Navy Act. *See* section 3(2), Navy Act.

Circumstances

Conditions, facts, etc. connected with an event or person.

Circumstantial Evidence

Evidence of a fact from which some other fact is inferred. It establishes commission of an offence by placing circumstances, which lead to an irresistible inference of guilt of accused, and are inconsistent with his innocence.

Citizen

Persons having full rights in a country, either by birth or by gaining such rights.

Civil Affair

Any question relating to relations in wartime between the commander of an armed force and the civilian populations and governments in areas where the force is employed, and which is settled on the basis of a mutual agreement, official or otherwise.

Civil Affairs and Military Government

(a) *Civil Affairs.* Civil affairs are the exercise of temporary military control by one State over the civilian population of another State by agreement, formal or otherwise.

(b) *Military Government*. Military control exercised by the armed occupying forces over enemy territory as a result of the military occupation of that territory.

Civil Airliner

Civil aircraft clearly identifiable as such and engaged in carrying civilian passenger in scheduled or non-scheduled service along Air Traffic Services routes.

See HPCR Draft Manual on Air and Missile Warfare.

Civil Custody

Custody of the police or other lawful civil authority authorised to retain in custody civil prisoners, and includes confinement in a civil prison. It means the custody of the police or in a civil prison.

Civil Defence

Performance of some or all of the undermentioned humanitarian tasks intended to protect the civilian population against the dangers and to help it to recover from the immediate effects of hostilities or disasters, and also to provide the conditions necessary for its survival. These tasks are:

(a) warning;

(b) evacuation;

(c) management of shelters;

(d) management of blackout measures;

(e) rescue;

(f) medical services, including first aid, and religious assistance;

(g) fire-fighting;

(h) detection and marking of danger areas;

(i) decontamination and similar protective measures;

(j) provision of emergency accommodation and supplies;

(k) emergency assistance in the restoration and maintenance of order in distressed areas;

(l) emergency repair of indispensable public utilities;

(m) emergency disposal of the dead;

(n) assistance in the preservation of objects essential for survival;

(o) complementary activities necessary to carry out any of the tasks mentioned above, including, but not limited to, planning and organisation;

[Article 61(1) – Protocol Additional to the Geneva Conventions of 12 August, 1949, and relating to the Protection of Victims of International Armed Conflicts (Protocol I), 8 June, 1977.]

Civil Defence Organisations

Those establishments and other units which are organised or authorised by the competent authorities of a Party to the conflict to perform any of the tasks mentioned under Article 61(1) and which are assigned and devoted exclusively to such tasks, and "Personnel" of civil defence organisations means those persons assigned by a Party to the conflict exclusively to the performance of the tasks mentioned under Article 61(1) including personnel assigned by the competent authority of that Party exclusively to the administration of these organisations.

[Article 61(2) – Protocol Additional to the Geneva Conventions of 12 August, 1949, and relating to the Protection of Victims of International Armed Conflicts (Protocol I), 8 June, 1977.]

Civilian

A civilian is any person who does not belong to one of the categories of persons referred to in Article 4A (1), (2), (3) and (6) of the Third Geneva Convention and in Article 43 of AP I. In case of doubt whether a person is a civilian, that person shall be considered to be a civilian. As a matter of principle, they enjoy a status of immunity under the International Humanitarian Law. *See* AP I, Article 50.

Civilians

Any person who is not a member of the armed forces is considered to be a civilian. *See* AP II Article 25(1). All persons who are not members of the military. Civilians lose their immunity if, and for the time that, they take a direct part in hostilities. *See* AP I, Article 51(3).

Civilian Objects

Are all objects that are not military objects.

Civil Area

An area declared to be a civil area by the Central Government under section 43A of the Cantonment Act, 1924.

Civil Authorities

This includes political and police authorities. *See* Note 2 to Army Act, section 105.

Civil Offence

A civil offence is one which is triable by a criminal court. *See* Army Act, section 3(ii), Navy Act, section 3(3).

Civil Prison

Civil prison means any jail or place used for the detention of any criminal prisoner under the Prisons Act, 1894, or under any other law for the time being in force. *See* Army Act, section 3(iii).

Civil War

War conducted largely within the boundaries of a State in which a significant part of the population is associated with opposing sides. One or both sides may have external help.

Claim

Right to demand, or has a right to. It is a demand for a transfer of ownership of money or property and does not include requisitions for the mere use of property.

Classified Matter

Official information or matter in any form or of any nature which requires protection in the interests of national security.

Clemency

Clemency is employed towards offenders and is arbitrary on the part of dispenser, flowing from his will, independent of the object on whom it is bestowed. Clemency lies in the disposition. Discretionary action by person authorised to reduce the severity of the sentence.

Clergyman

Is a minister, priest, rabbi, chaplain or other similar functionary of a religious organisation, or an individual reasonably believed to be so by the person consulting the clergyman. US MRE 503(b)(1).

Close Arrest

One of the forms of arrest, the other being open arrest. When arrest is not described by the authority ordering it as open arrest, it means close arrest. *See* RA(DSR), para 391(b).

Closed Court

A court-martial shall, where it is so directed by the Army Rules, and may in any other case on any deliberation amongst its members sit in closed court. Then only the members, the Judge Advocate and any officer under instruction are present – Army Rule 80.

Closing Address

The address made by the accused or his counsel or the defending officer (as the case may be) after the close of the case for the prosecution and when the accused has called his witnesses. *See* Army Rule 59(d).

Coalition

It is a temporary defence-related arrangement between two or more States for a particular end or purpose and without reference to wider application or employment of the arrangement.

Coarse

Rough, of poor quality, not fine. *See* Army Rule 77(3).

Co-Belligerency

(1) Status of armed forces falling short of recognition as the armed forces of a subject of international law. (2) Relation between belligerent States falling short of an alliance.

Code

A collection of rules and regulations which are sanctioned by the authority, for the better Government of the army, such as the Army Act.

Code of Military Law

It is laid down partly in acts of Parliament, and partly in Regulations made under the authority of those Acts or in accordance with the custom of the service.

Codification

(1) Restatement or reform of law in written form and with binding effect. (2) Synonym of restatement of law.

Coercive

Coercive circumstances need not be evidenced by a show of physical force. Threats, intimidation, extortion and other forms of duress which prey on fear or desperation may constitute coercion, and coercion may be inherent in certain circumstances, such as armed conflict or the military presence. [ICTR Judgment, *The Prosecutor* v. *Jean Paul Akayesu,* ICTR-96-4-T, para 688.]

Colour Service

The part of service by a combatant in regular Army after which he is liable to render reserve service.

Collateral

Subordinate effect not primarily intended.

Collateral Damage

It consists of unavoidable and unplanned damage to civilian personnel and property incurred while attacking a military objective. Also defined as damage to personnel and property adjacent to, but not forming part of, an authorised target.

Collective Act

Joint action taken by more than two States.

Collective Defence

Assistance given to a State acting in self-defence.

Collective Fine

Army Act, section 89 permits imposition of collective fines for the purpose of enforcing collective responsibility for losses of arms. Experience has shown that such responsibility is the best safeguard for the security of the arms of a company or similar unit. Collective fines cannot be imposed on officers but only on JCOs, WOs, NCOs and men of the company of equivalent unit concerned.

Collective Security

System of mutual assistance which is not directed against any particular State.

Collectively

In a collective manner or capacity.

Cognizant

Cognizance means judicial notice or knowledge; the judicial recognition or hearing of a cause. Legal right to deal with a matter, the hearing and trying of a cause.

Combat

Military combat is a contest in which the parties attempt to achieve mutually incompatible aims through the organised use of force by armed forces.

Combat Related Offences

These offences relate exclusively to combat situations. They are tailored to punishment of individuals who assist the enemy or engage in activities which might assist the enemy. These offences, due to their ramifications on the military mission, are often punishable by death.

Combatant

Members of the military armed forces of a party to a conflict (other than medical personnel and chaplains covered by Article 33 of the Third Convention) are combatants, that is to say, they have the right to participate directly in hostilities. *See* Article 43 to AP I. Whoever is a soldier in the armed forces of a State is a combatant. All persons who are not combatants are civilians. Combatants include: the regular armed forces of a State party to the conflict, militia, volunteer corps, and organised resistance movements belonging to a State party to the conflict that are under responsible command, wear a fixed distinctive sign recognisable at a distance, carry their arms openly and abide by the laws of war, and members of armed forces of a Government not recognised by a detaining authority or occupying power.

Combatant Immunity

It is the right of a combatant in an armed conflict to commit violent acts against hostile combatant forces within the limits of the laws of war.

Combatants

Members of the military who may take part in hostilities and are legitimate object of individualised attacks. Combatants are only protected from attack when they are *hors de combat* because they have surrendered, are sick or wounded and not carrying on the fight, are ship-wrecked or have parachuted from a disabled aircraft. They are also immune from attack when serving as parliamentarians conducting negotiations with the enemy or as medical or religious personnel.

Combatised Tradesman

A person appointed or in pay as a combatised tradesman. *See* section 2(1)(c) of the NSG Act, 1986.

Combination of Punishments

Under Army Act, section 73, two or more punishments applicable to the rank of the offender may be awarded in combination.

Command

(a) The authority vested in an individual of the armed forces for the direction, co-ordination and control of military forces. The authority that a commander in military service lawfully exercises over his/her subordinates by virtue of being placed in command by a superior officer.

(b) An order given by command; that is, the will of the commander expressed for purpose of bringing about a particular action.

(c) A unit, or units, an organisation, or an area under the command of one individual.

This also means one of the commands into which India is for military purpose for the time being divided, and includes any area which the Central Government may, by notification in the Official Gazette, declare to be a command for all or any of the purposes of this Act. *See* section 2(viii) of the Cantonments Act, 1924.

Commander

An officer who has the command of a garrison, fort, castle, regiment, company or formation etc.

Commander-in-Chief

The officer commanding-in-chief of the regular army; the supreme military commander of the entire forces of the State.

Command Influence

The improper influence by a superior in command with the independent judgment of persons responsible for judicial decisions. Command influence is said to be mortal enemy of military justice. Unlawful command influence can be either actual or apparent.

Command Responsibility

Commanders are legally responsible for war crimes committed by their subordinates when any of three circumstances apply:—

(a) the commander ordered the commission of the act;

(b) the commander knew of the act, either before or during its commission, and did nothing to prevent or stop it; or

(c) the commander should have known through reports received by him or through other means that troops or other persons subject to his control were about to commit or had committed a war crime and he failed to take the necessary and reasonable steps to ensure compliance with the law of war or to punish violators thereof.

Commanding Officer

When used in any provisions of the Army Act, with reference to any separate portion of the regular Army or to any department thereof, means the officer whose duty it is under the regulations of the regular Army, or in the absence of any such regulations, by the custom of the service to discharge with respect to that portion of the regular Army or that department, as the case may be, the functions of a commanding officer in regard to matters of the description referred to in that provision. *See* Army Act, section 3(v).

Commencement

Beginning of something.

Commission

A written order giving a person rank and authority as an officer in the armed forces.

Commissioned Officer

An officer who has been granted a commission in the armed services, *i.e.*, any person appointed to a rank of Second Lieutenant or higher in the Army, Navy or Air Force. Under the Navy Act, section 3(5), it means a person holding a commission from the President in the Indian Navy or the Indian Naval Reserve Forces.

Committal

To consign to custody by official warrant, to send to prison, to imprison, to be put in any place to be kept safe.

Committal Order

The order made by the Commanding Officer or other prescribed officer to the appropriate civil jail after confirmation of a sentence of imprisonment passed by a court-martial accompanied by dismissal where the prisoner is sent under police escort. [RA(DSR), paras 511 and 512.]

Committee of Adjustment

It is convened to make up the non-effective account of a deceased soldier. It will, as soon as possible, secure and make an inventory of all his personal effects, in camp or quarters at home.

Common Intent

If several persons combined together for an unlawful purpose or for a lawful purpose to be effected by unlawful means, each is responsible for every offence committed by any of them in furtherance of that purpose. *See* IPC, section 34.

Common Law Forgery

It consists of the fraudulent making or alteration of a document or writing to the prejudice of another person's right.

Communicates

To bestow, convey, make known, recount, to import as to communicate information to anyone. The transit information. *See* Army Act, section 34(d).

Commutation

A substitution of a less thing for a greater, the substitution of a lesser punishment for a greater one. It is changing the description of punishment by awarding a punishment lower in the scale of punishment.

Company

A body of men in one or more platoons, forming one of the principal divisions and the first unit of an infantry battalion.

Company Conduct Sheets

It is kept for every non-Commissioned Officer and man in the company in a guard book by the Company commander in his own possession. In it is to be recorded every offence committed by any man for which punishment has been awarded or reprimand administered. On promotion to a rank higher than NCO, or on discharge, a man's Company Conduct Sheet will be destroyed.

Compassionate Exemption

In the context of entry into the military, means, where the father or one or more sons or daughters of a family were killed in action or died in line of duty while serving in the Armed Forces, the sole surviving son of such family shall not be inducted for service. Section 6(o) of the Selective Services Act, 1948, of the USA.

Complaint

It is an allegation that a wrong has been done or a grievance suffered. It is the form of a formal process which consists of an allegation against a superior, made or presented to the appropriate officer, as for a wrong done. It is an utterance of grievance.

Compensation

Anyone who has been the victim of unlawful arrest or detention shall have an enforceable right to compensation. *See* Article 85 of the ICC Statute.

Compensation, Principle of

A State itself is liable for violations of the law of war committed by citizens acting on behalf of the State.

Competent

Answering to all requirements, adequate, sufficient, suitable, capable, legally qualified.

Competent Authority

The Government or any other authority to which relevant powers may be delegated by the Government. *See* Financial Regulations, Part I, section 1. Having the power to decide something. *See* Army Act, section 102(4).

Competent Financial Authority

The authority within whose financial powers the amount at issue falls. *See* Financial Regulations, Part I, section 1.

Complete

Whole, total, opposite of incomplete. *See* Army Act, section 26(3).

Complete Termination

It refers to a discharge relieving the service member of any further military service.

Composition

Formation or construction. The term is used in conjunction of the formation of a court-martial.

Compromised

A term applied to classified matter, knowledge of which has, in whole or in part, passed to unauthorised person or persons, or which has been subject to risk of such passing.

Compulsion

Or inevitable necessity is a constraint upon the will whereby an officer is urged to that which his judgment disapproves, and which it is to be presumed, his will (if left to itself) would reject.

Compulsorily

Mandatory. Opposite of voluntarily. *See* Army Rule 13A.

Compulsory Retirement

Army Rules provision contain the contingency when officers shall be liable to be compulsorily retired from service by order of the Central Government on attaining the age limit specified. Army Rule 16A.

Computation

To calculate something. *See* Army Act, section 185.

Concentration of Civilians

Any concentration of civilians, be it permanent or temporary, such as in inhabited parts of cities, or inhabited town or villages, or as in camps or columns of refugees or evacuees, or groups of nomads.

[Article 1(2), Protocol on Prohibitions or Restrictions on the Use of Incendiary Weapons (Protocol III), Geneva, 10 October 1980.]

Concept of Violence

For the purpose of military criminal law, violence includes murder, either attempted or actual, personal injury, battery, cruelty and any attempt to inflict injury with a weapon. *See* Article 43 CPMP.

Concession Voucher

Usually refers to a military certificate form which provides for concession for defence service personnel travelling on leave.

Conciliatory

One who brings opponents into harmony, having the intention or effect of making angry people calm. *See* RA(DSR), para 546.

Conclusive Proof

When one fact is declared by the Indian Evidence Act to be conclusive proof of another, the court shall, on proof of the one fact, regard the other as proved, and shall not allow evidence to be given for the purpose of disproving it. *See* section 3 of the Indian Evidence Act, 1872.

Concur

To agree, coincide, express agreement in opinion.

Concurrence

The action of concurring. *See* Army Act, section 132(3).

Concurrent Jurisdiction

The word 'concurrent' means having the same authority.

A criminal court and a court-martial may each have jurisdiction in respect of same offence. Adjustment of jurisdiction is provided for by Army Act, sections 125 and 126, which give the military authorities the right of deciding by which court the alleged offender is to be tried.

Concurrently

Existing or happening at the same time. *See* Army Act, section 188.

Conditions

Thing on whose fulfilment another thing or act is made to depend. It is something agreed upon as a requisite to the doing or taking effect of something else. *See* Army Act, sections 8(2) and 179.

Condonation

It is deliberate overlooking of an offence by competent authority, done well with full knowledge of all material facts. It bars subsequent trial by court-martial or summary disposal. *See* Army Rule 53(i)(b). No authority lower than COAS is competent to condone.

Condone

To forgive or overlook an offence.

Conduct

It is used with reference to the character or reputation of the individual.

Conduct Sheet

It is prepared and maintained for every person subject to the Army Act. The conduct sheet of officers, JCOs and WOs will be kept as confidential documents, those of NCOs and men will be kept with other service documents. For the entries and in what colour ink are the same to be made in conduct sheets. *See* RA(DSR), paras 386 and 387.

Confession

It is a statement of the accused which, either admits in terms of the offence, or at any rate substantially all the facts which constitute the offence, and made by a person accused of an offence, *i.e.*, when a formal accusation relating to commission of an offence had been levelled which in the normal course might result in prosecution. It must either admit in terms the offence, or at any rate substantially all the facts which constitute the offence.

Confidential Report

These are reports on all officers as per laid down procedure and for special purposes in accordance with the instructions issued by the Chief of the Army Staff from time to time. *See* RA(DSR), para 106.

Confinement

It is being placed in charge of a guard, picquet, patrol, sentry or provost marshal. It is applicable only in case of sepoys. It includes confinement in unit quarter guard while undergoing a sentence of imprisonment or detention. A person in confinement loses pay and allowances. *See* RA(DSR), paras 394(c), 395(b), Note 16 to Army Section 3 and Note 8 to Army Act, section 91. Confinement is the most severe pre-trial restriction on the accused's freedom as it involves incarceration or placement of a guard over the accused.

Confinement to lines

One of the punishments awardable to a sepoy by way of summary trial. This will entail a defaulter required to answer to his name at uncertain hours throughout the day, and employed on working parties to fullest practicable extent. He will attend parade and take all duties in regular turn. He may be ordered to attend extra drill upto one hour a day. *See* Note 11 to Army Act, section 80 and item 1 of Table to RA(DSR), para 443.

Confirmation

The act of confirmation. In military law sense, the term denotes confirmation of the finding, and, of sentence of a court-martial. It is carried out by an officer or authority called confirming officer or authority.

Confiscation

The appropriation to the public use of private property. A right which is conferred under certain circumstances by the laws of war.

Conflict

It is a situation of confrontation existing between groups, classes or States in which violence is either manifested or threatened.

Conjointly

Related to, made up of or carried on by two or more in combination. *See* Army Act, section 81(3).

Conquest

Forcible occupation of enemy territory.

Conscience

The sense of right and wrong that governs a person's thoughts and actions and deligence. *See* Army Rules 9, 45 and 46.

Consceintions Objection

In the context of entry into military service means exemption from conscription those who by reason of religious training or belief are opposed to participation in war in any form. There is one caveat. Whatever the registrant's belief, they must be sincerely held to qualify for the exemption. [Section 6(j) of the Universal Military Training and Service Act, of USA.]

Conscript

To compel to military service by conscription, to enlist compulsorily.

Conscription

A basic route into military service is based on the Parliament's (US Congress) power to raise and support armies. The term is defined as enrolment or enlistment of soldiers. To force someone by law to serve in one of the armed forces; compulsory enlistment for State Service, especially military service.

Consecutive

Following in uninterrupted succession.

Consent

Voluntary agreement by a person in the possession and exercise of sufficient mental capacity to make an intelligent choice to do something proposed by another. It is an act unclouded by fraud, duress, or sometimes even mistake.

Consequence

A result or effect, an inference reached by reasoning; conclusion. *See* Army Act, section 68.

Consistency

The quality of always behaving in the same way or of having the same opinion, standard etc.

Consistent

Happening in the same way and continuing for a period of time.

Conspiracy
It consists in the agreement of two or more persons to do an unlawful act or do a lawful act by unlawful means.

Constable
Includes a high constable and a commissioner, inspector or other officer of police.

Constructive Desertion
An act where the intention of the accused is to avoid some important military duty.

Constructive Enlistment
Article 2(b) of the Uniform Code of Military Justice validates for jurisdictional purposes the enlistment of "any person who has the capacity to understand the significance of enlisting".

Constructive Knowledge
The doctrine that a commander has an affirmative duty to take measures necessary to protect prisoners of war and civilians. Knowledge which may be found to have existed because the regulation, notice, fact, or directive at issue was of so notorious a nature, or was so conspicuously posted or distributed, that the particular accused ought to have known of its existence.

Consult
It implies a conference of two or more persons or the impact of two or more minds brought about in respect of a topic with a view to evolve a correct or at least a satisfactory solution. *See* Army Rule 49.

Consultation
It is a conference between the persons engaged in a case, to discuss its questions or arrange the method of conducting it.

Consumables
Supplies of a general nature, consumed on a routine basis, consumables include combat supplies, general and technical stores, ammunition and other basic commodities in support of major equipment as well as in support of minor equipment and personnel.

Contempt

A wilful disregard or disobedience of superior authority, a mental attitude in which a thing is considered as vile and worthless.

Contemptuous

Showing or feeling contempt, disdainful.

Contents of Charge

Every charge shall be divided into two parts:—

(a) statements of the offence.

(b) statements of the particulars of the act, neglect or omission constituting the offence. *See* Army Rule 30.

Contiguity

Claim to neighbouring territory based on proximity.

Contingent

All formed units personnel and equipment of the troop contributing country deployed to the mission area of the United Nations peacekeeping operation under a memorandum.

Contingent Allowance

A sum paid periodically to each commander to defray the expense of stationery, the care of arms, and the other minor demands. Also the account sent by a staff officer of money expended for miscellaneous purposes.

Continuity

Logical sequence, continuous or connected whole.

Contraband

Goods which are ultimately destined for territory under the control of an enemy belligerent party, which are susceptible for use in international armed conflict and which are contained in contraband lists.

See HPCR Draft Manual on Air and Missile Warfare.

Contract

An agreement between two or more persons who are legally capable of making a binding agreement, which involves a promise (or set of promises), a consideration (*i.e.*, something of value promised or given), a reasonable amount of understanding between the persons as to what the agreement means, and a legal means for resolving any breach of the agreement.

Contract Administration

All the activities associated with the performance of a contract, from pre-award to close out.

Contract Authority

Budgetary authority contained in an authorisation bill that permits an agency of the concerned Government to enter into contracts or other obligations for future payments from funds not yet appropriated by the Parliament.

Contract Requirements

In addition to specified performance requirements, contract requirements include those defined in the statement of work, specifications, standards, and related documents – the contract data requirement list, management systems, and contract terms and conditions.

Contract Termination

Cessation or cancellation, in whole or in part, of work under a prime contract, or a sub-contract thereunder, for the convenience of, or at the option of, the Government, or a foreign purchaser, or due to failure of the contractor to perform in accordance with the terms of the contract.

Contractual Period

The period mentioned in the enrolment form (IAFK 1162) in respect of general duty personnel and other ranks.

Contrary

Opposite of what is expected. *See* Army Act, section 145(1).

Contrary to law

Violating or not conforming to the provision of law.

Controlling Officer

An officer who is entrusted with the responsibility of controlling the progress of expenditure under any appropriation. *See* Financial Regulations, Part-I, section 1.

Convening Authority

The Convening Authority is a person authorised by the UCMJ to create a court-martial by assigning members of the court and referring charges to it. The persons so authorised vary depending upon the type of court-martial convened.

Convening Order

Once it is decided that an accused will be tried by court-martial, an order for assembly of the court, known as convening order, is issued. This order is signed by the Convening Officer. It designates the kind of court, place and time it is to meet, members of the court, and the authority by which the court-martial is created.

Convention

An official agreement between countries.

Conventional War

It conforms, most closely, to the traditional image of war and is fought to achieve strategic and military objectives. It does not include the use of WMD *i.e.*, NBC weapons. These can be initiated either in a pro-active or reactive mode.

Convert

The process when a soldier is allowed by the competent authority to change his colour service into reserve service, and thus be transferred to the Reserve sooner than he had agreed on enlistment. This is a privilege and cannot be claimed.

Conveyance

In military sense is used to denote a means of transport.

Convicted

The past record of having been guilty of an offence against the law or a person who had served a prison sentence.

Cordon

A chain of military or police piquets organised to control movement into and out of a guarded area.

Corps

Any separate body of persons subject to the Army Act which is prescribed as a corps for the purposes of all or any of the provisions of the said Act. *See* Army Act, section 3(vi).

Corps Staff Appointment

Appointments dealing with matters connected with an individual Corps or Service and tenable by officers of that Corps or Service only. [RA(DSR) – explanation of terms used.]

Correspondence

The letters a person sends and receives, the activity of writing letters. *See* Army Act, section 35(b).

Corruption

Dishonest or illegal behaviour, especially of people in authority. *See* Army Act, section 53.

Cost Contract

A contract which provides for payments to the contractor of allowable costs, to the extent prescribed in the contract, incurred in the performance of the contract.

Cost Estimate

A judgment or opinion regarding the anticipated cost of an object, commodity or service. A cost estimate is the result of an estimated procedure which specifies the expected currency cost required to perform a stipulated task or to acquire an item. A cost estimate may constitute a single value or a range of values.

Cost Sharing Contract

A cost sharing reimbursement type contract under which the contractor receives no fee and is reimbursed only for the agreed portion of the allowable costs prescribed in the contract.

Counterfeit

A likeness or resemblance intended to deceive and to be taken for that which is original and genuine. A person is said to counterfeit who causes one thing to resemble another thing, intending by means of that resemblance to practice deception, or knowing it to be likely that deception will thereby be practiced. *See* section 28 of the Indian Penal Code.

Counter Insurgency

All the measures of Government activity to combat insurgency, including operations of the military, para-military and civil police force, economic development, political reforms and psychological warfare aimed at winning the hearts and minds of the people.

Countersign

To sign what has already been signed by a superior, to authenticate by an additional signature.

Counter Terrorism

Counter terrorism covers all offensive measures taken to respond to terrorist acts and could include actions taken by all Government agencies, including the Security Forces of a nation. The measures could be in terms of bringing terrorists to justice or their elimination by direct action, isolation and application of pressure on states that sponsor terrorism, amongst other measures.

Court

It includes all judges and magistrates, and all persons, except arbitrators legally authorised to take evidence. *See* section 3 of the Indian Evidence Act, 1872.

Court-Fee

A fee received under the Court-fees Act on plaints, petitions etc. *See* RA(DSR), para 535.

Court-Martial

A court consisting of officers of the Army, Navy or Air Force for the trial of offences against military law. There are general courts-martial, district court-martial, summary general court-martial and summary court-martial. A military tribunal composed of one or more members of the Armed Forces.

Court-Martial Box

It is a box to be kept by all holders of Courts-martial warrant, officer commanding stations and units, containing books and pamphlets as specified in RA(DSR), para 612 for use of members of all the Courts-martial.

Court of Appeals for the Armed Forces

A civilian appellate court composed of five judges appointed by the President and confirmed by the Senate under UCMJ.

Court of Criminal Appeals

A military appellate court composed of not less than three officers or civilians that reviews records of certain courts-martial under UCMJ.

Court of Inquest

Necessary formalities carried out in cases of unnatural death, *i.e.*, deaths due to suicide, violence, accident or under suspicious circumstances. The responsibility for holding it devolves on the local civil authorities in accordance with the provisions of section 174 of the Cr PC, 1973. Where the civil authorities are not easily accessible, as for instance in operational areas, and it is not practicable for them to hold an inquest before the dead body may become putrefied, a general approval for conducting military courts of inquest may be obtained in advance from State Governments concerned.

Court of Inquiry

It is an assembly of officers or of one or more officers with one or more JCOs, WOs and/or NCOs directed to collect and record evidence, and if so required, to report with regard to any matters referred to it. *See* Army Rule 177(1) and RA(DSR), para 518.

Court of Justice

The words denote a judge who is empowered by law to act judicially alone, or a body of judges which is empowered by law to act judicially as a body, when such judge or body of judges is acting judicially. *See* section 20 of the Indian Penal Code.

Court of Military Appeal

A court composed of three civilian judges appointed by the President and confirmed by the Senate, to act as Supreme Court of Appeals on decisions of Boards of Review.

Court Witness

The court may call any witness at any time before the finding if it considers that it is necessary for the ends of justice. *See* Army Rule 143(4).

Cowardice

Lack of courage in facing danger, pain or difficulty. It is misbehaviour motivated by fear.

Crime

A felony or misdeameanour, and does not include breach of contract.

Crimes Against Humanity

One of the most serious crimes of concern to the international community as a whole, as included in Article 7 to the ICC Statute. It would so amount, when committed as part of a widespread or systematic attack directed against any civilian population, with the knowledge of the attack.

Criminal Breach of Trust

Whoever, being in any manner entrusted with property, or with any dominion over property, dishonestly misappropriates or converts to his own use that property, or dishonestly uses or disposes of that property in violation of any direction of law prescribing the mode in which such trust is to be discharged, or of any legal contract, express or implied, which he has made touching the discharge of such trust or wilfully suffers any other person so to do, commits "criminal breach of trust". *See* section 405 of the Indian Penal Code.

Criminal Court

It means a court of ordinary criminal justice in any part of India. *See* section 3(viii) of the Army Act, 1950.

Criminal Force

Whoever intentionally uses force to any person without that person's consent, in order to the committing of any offence, or intending by the use of such force to cause, or knowing it to be likely that by the use of such force he will cause injury, fear or annoyance to the person to whom the force is used, is said to use criminal force. *See* Army Act, sections 40(a), 42(b) and 47 etc.

Criminality

The fact of people being involved in crime, criminal acts.

Criminalize

To make something illegal by passing a new law.

Crisis

A situation, which may or may not be foreseen, which threatens security or interests or peace and stability, and which requires decision and action.

Criteria Appointments

These are specified appointments in which an officer must earn reports for the laid down adequately exercised period before he can be awarded a definite grading for promotion by the selection board.

Cross-Examination

It is examination of the witness by the opposite party.

Cruel Treatment

Is treatment which causes serious mental or physical suffering or constitutes a serious attack upon human dignity which is equivalent to the offence of inhuman treatment in the framework of the grave breaches provisions of the Geneva Conventions. [ICTY Judgment, *The Prosecutor* v. *Zejnil Delalic and others*, IT-96-21-T, para 551.]

Cruelty

Infliction of suffering for the sake of suffering or for revenge. Cruelty usually involves the doing of some positive act, such as beating or killing or torturing. *See* Army Act, section 46(a). But there are circumstances in which cruelty can be charged against a person who has culpably failed to do what he ought to have done.

Culpability

Doctrine according to which an illegal act requires guilt (intent or negligence).

Culpable Inefficiency

Is inefficiency for which there is no reasonable or just excuse.

Culpable Neglect

It is failure to exercise that reasonable and proper care and to take precautions to guard against injury either to the public generally or to an individual in particular which, having regard to all the circumstances attending the charge it was the imperative duty of the accused person to have adopted.

Cultural Property

Movable or immovable property dedicated to religion, art, science, education or charitable purposes, and historical monuments.

See HPCR Draft Manual on Air and Missile Warfare.

Cultural Property of Great Importance to Human Heritage

Monuments of architecture, art, history, religion or archeological sites whose value transcends geographical boundaries, or which are unique in character and are intimately associated with the history and culture of a people.

See HPCR Draft Manual on Air and Missile Warfare.

Curfew

A measure to prohibit people and vehicles from travelling and operating at certain hours in certain areas, excluding cases permitted under regulations of the persons competent to organise the realization of a curfew order. Article 310 of the Vietnam's Law on National Defence.

Custody

When a person is held by law enforcement or investigating authorities or the judicial custody. It means the actual or physical holding. It is restraint of free locomotion imposed by lawful apprehension. The restraint may be physical or, once there has been a submission to apprehension or a forcible taking into custody, it may consist of control exercised in the presence of the prisoner by official acts or orders.

Custom

It arises out of long established practices which by common usage have attained the force of law in the military or other community affected by them. No custom may be contrary to existing law or regulation. A custom which has not been adopted by existing statute or regulation ceases to exist when its observance has been generally abandoned.

Customs of the Service

Signifies generally a right or law not written, but established by long usage. To render a custom valid, it has been said that the following requisites are needed:
(1) It must have been used so long that the memory of man runs not to the contrary; (2) it must have been continued; (3) peaceable; also (4) reasonable; (5) certain; (6) compulsory, and not left to the options of every person, whether he will use it or not; and (7) consistent with other customs, for one custom cannot be set up in opposition to another.

Customs of War

By these customs, for the most part tacitly, or in some cases explicitly, agreed on between civilized nations, the commander of an Army in occupation of a foreign country governs his own troops by the military law of his country, while he imposes such laws and regulations on the inhabitants as he deems necessary for the security of his forces and the maintenance of good order among the population.

Customary Law

A custom which by continuance has acquired the force of law.

Cut-Off Year

Refers to the reporting year of the last report which is taken into consideration for promotion to the next higher rank.

D

Damage
Injury suffered from an illegal act.

Damages
Indemnity for injury suffered from an illegal act.

Death
Death occurring in the specified area of operational responsibilities due to enemy action. It also includes death in harness in the performance of duties due to accident, act of violence by terrorist or anti social elements, border skirmishes, action against militants etc. *See* rule 2 of the Punjab War Heroes Families Relief Fund.

Debt Conciliatory Board
The provisions contained in RA(DSR), para 546 make it obligatory for a JCO, WO or serving OR who is a creditor or debtor and has occasion to appoint an agent or *mukhtiar* to obtain prior sanction of the board.

Debtor
A person who owes another anything. *See* RA(DSR), para 838.

Deceit
Fraud, false representation made with intent to deceive, guile. Deceipt is indeterminate when compared with fraud, which is a specific mode of deceiving. *See* Note 24 to Army Act, section 52.

Deceive
To deceive is to induce a man to believe a thing as true which is false, and which the person practicing the deceit knows, or believes to be false.

Deception
Is a conscious and deliberate effort to mislead an adversary by subtle misrepresentation to gain a competitive advantage.

Declaration
An official or formal statement, a written or spoken statement. *See* Army Rule 36.

Decoration

A badge, medal, clasp, good conduct badge, ribbon or cross etc. bestowed for distinguished services or gallantry.

Decree

The final order of a court in a suit. *See* RA(DSR), para 533(c).

Deduction

Act of deducing, inference from the general to the particular, of lowering the aggregate or capital sum or quantity. *See* Army Act, section 25.

Default

Failure to do something that must be done by law. *See* Army Act, section 59(a).

Defaulter

One who fails to perform a duty, a delinquent, who fails to account for public money entrusted to his care. *See* Army Rule 143(3).

Defence Civilians

Refers to the civilian personnel who are paid from the defence services estimate and are on the pay rolls of the Central Government.

Defence Counsel

Is a counsel who is engaged by or for one or more accused persons to represent them at their trial by court-martial. Under UCMJ, a judge advocate who represents a military member in any adverse actions.

Defence Estate Officer

The officer appointed by the Central Government to perform the duties of the Defence Estate Officer for the purposes of the Cantonment Act, 1924 and the Rules made thereunder.

Defendant

The person in a trial who is accused of committing a crime, or who is being sued by another person. *See* RA(DSR), para 538.

Defending Officer

An officer subject to military law who represents an accused at a trial by court-martial.

Deferments

Temporary relief from military duty in the context of conscription.

Deferred

An officer is not eligible for suitable assessment if he is not adequately exercised. He is awarded the grading 'Deferred'.

Deficient

Not having enough of something, especially something that is essential.

Defiling

Making something dirty or no longer pure; especially something that people consider important or holy. *See* Army Act, section 64(b).

Definite Grading

This refers to the grading which can be awarded by the selection board screening the officers for promotion to the next higher rank. The following are the definite grading:—

(a) B. The officer is fit for promotion in his own turn to the next higher rank.

(b) Z. The officer is non empanelled for promotion to the next higher rank at present.

Defraud

To defraud is to deprive by deceit, or to induce a man to act to his injury.

Defray

To give somebody back the money that they have spent on something. *See* Army Rule 137.

Degrading Treatment

Treatment or punishment of an individual may be said to be degrading if it grossly humiliates him before others or drives him to act against his will or conscience. *See* European Convention on Human Rights.

Delay Report

It is a report submitted by the commanding officer when an accused has remained in custody for a period longer than eight days without court-martial for his trial having been ordered to assemble. It is submitted in the form given in Appendix III, Part IV to the Army Rules. *See* Army Rule 27(1).

Delegation

The act of making or commissioning a delegate, parting with authority, the transfer of authority by one person to another. *See* RA(DSR), para 816.

Deliberate

Premeditated, not sudden or rash, to weigh in the mind, to consider and examine the reasons for and against. *See* Army Rule 105(5).

Deliver

Actual, constructive, or attempted transfer of an item, whether or not there exists an agency relationship.

Demilitarised Zones

A defended area in which the stationing or concentrating of military forces, or the retention or establishment of military installations of any description is prohibited.

Demonstration

Public meeting or march at which people show that they are protesting against or supporting somebody or something. *See* Army Act, section 21.

Department

It includes any division or branch of a department. *See* section 3(ix) of the Army Act.

Dependents

A person who depends on another person for a home, food etc.

Deportation

Deportation or forcible transfer of population means forced displacement of the persons concerned by expulsion or other coercive acts from the area in which they are lawfully present, without grounds permitted under international law. *See* Article 7.2(d) of the ICC Statute.

Deposition

A formal statement, taken from somebody and used in a court of law. *See* Army Act, section 138(3).

Deprived

To prevent somebody from having or doing something, especially something important.

Derelict

A person is derelict in the performance of duties when that person wilfully or negligently fails to perform that person's duties or when that person performs them in a culpably inefficient manner.

Dereliction of Duty

Wilfully or negligently failing to perform assigned duties or performing them in a culpably inefficient manner.

Derogation

The act of annulling or breaking a law, or some part of it; partial surrender of a right. *See* Army Act, section 189.

Descent

Derivation from an ancestor, a person's family origins. *See* Army Rule, Appendix I, Form I.

Deserter Recruits

The recruits who desert after enrolment by the recruiting staff but before joining the unit to which posted. *See* RA(DSR), para 380.

Desertion

A serious military offence which implies an intention on the part of the accused either (a) never to return to the service, or (b) to avoid some important military duty (commonly known as constructive desertion). *See* Note 2 to Army Act, section 38. Under section 88(2) of Canada's National Defence Act, 1985, a person deserts who:

(a) being on or having been warned for active service duty during an emergency or other important service, is absent without authority with the intention of avoiding that service;

(b) having been warned that his vessel is under sailing orders, is absent without authority with the intention of missing that vessel;

(c) absents himself without authority from his place of duty with the intention of remaining absent from his place of duty;

(d) is absent without authority from his place of duty and at any time during such absence forms the intention of remaining absent from his place of duty; or

(e) while absent with authority from his place of duty, with the intention of remaining absent from his place of duty, does any act or omits to do anything, the natural and probable consequence of which act or omission is to preclude the person from being at his place of duty at the time required.

Designation

Distinctive title, appellation, that which serves to distinguish, a descriptive name. *See* Army Act, section 2(xviii).

Design

On purpose, intentionally, or according to a plan and requires specific intent.

Dispatch

Haste, to send off. *See* Army Act, section 168.

Despondency

Sad, without much hope. *See* Army Act, section 36(e).

Destruction of Property

To set fire to property, to destroy, to pull down, mutilate or damage.

Detachment

Every separate body of persons subject to the Army Act which is not a Corps or department is a detachment. *See* Note 2 to Army Act, section 16. A part of a unit separated from its main organization for duty elsewhere or temporary military unit formed from other units, or parts of units.

Detail

To order a person to perform a specific temporary duty, unless the context indicates otherwise. *See* Army Rule 151.

Detainee

Refers to any person captured or otherwise detained by armed force.

Detained Person

Any person deprived of personal liberty, except as a result of conviction for an offence. *See* Body of Principles for the

Protection of All persons Under Any Form of Detention or Imprisonment, adopted by the UN GA Resolution 43/173 of 9 Dec 1988.

Detenticn

One of the punishments awardable to a Sepoy by way of summary trial. It is a red ink entry. The defaulter is subjected to same restrictions as one undergoing rigorous imprisonment. He will not forfeit pay and allowances for the period of detention. He will do normal military training, in addition to any collective training that may be imposed. *See* RA(DSR), paras 510 and 387(b). It also means that act of holding in custody for lawful purposes such as prosecution, maintenance of public safety, or pursuant to legal order.

Detention Barrack

A building or part of a building set apart as such.

Detriment

The act of causing harm or damage. *See* Army Act, section 120(2).

Deviation

The act of moving away from what is normal or acceptable. *See* Army Rule 4.

Direct Evidence

It is the testimony of a witness as to the existence or non-existence of a fact in issue, as actually perceived by a witness by means of his own sense. It includes production of an original document. It excludes hearsay.

Direction

Instructions about how to do something. It contains most of instructions in it. Means guidance or command. *See* Army Act, section 87.

Disability

To incapacitate, make unable to act, to do something which creates a permanent disability. It is a deprivation of ability. Denotes solely the actual wound, injury or disease, the disablement caused by which gives rise to a claim for compensation. It is to be carefully distinguished from disablement which means physical or mental injury or damage, or loss of physical or mental capacity suffered by reason of a disability or disabilities.

Disability Pension

It is not a regular pension but is a casualty award, compensation for any disability caused during the performance of duties of service. Before an award can be made for a disability claimed, the same should be related to service and at least a casual connection must be established between disability and military service. [See *Pemmaiak MS, Ex Naik* v. *Union of India,* Mil LJ 1998 Kar 125]. It consists of service and disability elements and is admissible under the conditions as specified in various regulations.

Disadvantage

Something that causes problems and tends to stop somebody/ something from succeeding or making progress. *See* Army Rule 105(7).

Disappearance

The 'disappeared' are people who have been taken into custody by agents of the State, yet whose whereabouts and fate are concealed, and whose custody is denied.

Disband

The dismissal of a Regiment, or any large body of men, from the conditions of their military service, for disaffection or treasonable conduct.

Disbandment

The act of breaking up or dissolving an organization. *See* RA(DSR), para 838.

Disbursements (gross and net)

To pay money to somebody from a large amount that has been collected for a purpose. *See* RA(DSR), paras 804, 810 and 836(b). In budgetary usage, gross disbursements represent the amount of cheques issued, cash or other payments made, less refunds received. Net disbursements represent gross disbursements less income collected and credited to the appropriate fund account, such as amounts received for goods and services provided.

Disbursing Officer

A head of office or any other gazetted officer designated by a Department of the Central Government, a Head of Department or an Administration, to draw bills and make payments on behalf of the Government.

Discharge

The term pertains to JCOs, WOs and OR *vide* Army Rule 13 and is an administrative measure bringing service to an end. Discharge of an individual cannot be cancelled without his consent. *See* Army Rules 11(2) and 168. A soldier is entitled to be discharged on the termination of the period for which he engaged or re-engaged, except when his service is prolonged.

Discharge Certificate

A document furnished by a Commanding Officer to every JCO, WO or enrolled person who is dismissed, removed, discharged or released from the service, in the language which is the mother tongue of such person and also in English. It sets forth the authority terminating his service, the cause for such termination; and the full period of his service in the regularly Army. *See* Army Act, section 23.

Discharge with Disgrace

Discharged with ignominy, discharged for misconduct, or discharged on account of conviction for felony or of a sentence of penal servitude.

Discipline

The authoritative declared laws, rules and regulations for the guidance of all men and matters; the obedience to, and exercise of those laws; co-operative and active obedience to the orders and command of one's superior officers.

Discourage

To try to prevent something or to prevent somebody from doing something. *See* Army Act, section 34(b).

Discrepancy

Difference between two or more things that should be the same. *See* RA(DSR), para 809(a).

Discretion

The word signifies unrestrained exercise of choice or will; freedom to act according to one's own judgment. *See* Army Act, sections 125, 143(3) and 166.

Disgraceful Conduct

This term when used in conjunction with 'of an unnatural kind' means having, or attempting to have, carnal intercourse against the order of nature with a man, woman or animal. *See* Note 4 to Army Act, section 46 read with IPC, section 377.

Dishonestly

Whoever does anything with the intention of causing wrongful gain to one person or wrongful loss to another person, is said to do that thing 'dishonestly'. *See* section 24 of the Indian Penal Code.

Dishonourable Discharge

The most severe punitive discharge, reserved for those who should be separated under conditions of dishonour, after having been convicted of offences usually recognised by the civil law as felonies or military offences requiring severe punishment under UCMJ.

Dismissal

Dismissal is a court-martial punishment *vide* Army Act, section 71(e). It can be carried out as administrative measure as well. *See* Army Act, sections 19 and 20. Dismissal unlike discharge, is a bar to further Government service. *See* RA(DSR), para 168(c).

Dismissal of Charge

A charge may be dismissed by the commanding officer either before or after recording of summary of evidence. He must do so if there is no evidence of any offence under the Act and may do so if he considers that the evidence is doubtful or the case is trivial. *See* Notes to Army Rules 22 and 24.

Disorderly Conduct

It is conduct of such a nature as to affect the peace and quiet of persons who may witness it and who may be disturbed or provoked to resentment thereby. It includes conduct that endangers public morals or outrages public decency and any disturbance of a contentious or turbulent character.

Dispense

Not insist upon. *See* Army Rule 22(1).

Displeasure

It is one of the forms of censure conveyed in writing by a senior commander to a subordinate.

Dispose

To deal with a problem, question, threat or case successfully. *See* Army Rule 22(3).

Disproved

A fact is said to be disproved when, after considering the matters before it, the court either believes that it does not exist, or considers its non-existence so probable that a prudent man ought, under the circumstances of the particular case, to act upon the supposition that it does not exist. *See* section 3 of the Indian Evidence Act.

Disqualification

The term is used with reference to personal qualification of an officer to serve as a member of a court-martial. *See* Army Rule 39(2) for various grounds which incapacitate an officer.

Disqualified

This term is used with reference to the personal qualifications of an officer to serve on a court-martial. *See* Note 2 to Army Rule 39.

Disrespect

Disrespectful behaviour is that which detracts from the respect due the authority and person of a superior commissioned officer. It may consist of acts or language, however expressed, and it is immaterial whether they refer to the superior as an officer or as a private individual. Disrespect by words may be conveyed by abusive epithets or other contemptuous language. Truth is no defence. Disrespect by acts includes neglecting the customary salute, or showing a marked disdain, indifference, insolence, impertinence, undue familiarity, or other rudeness in the presence of the superior officer. Words, acts, omissions that are synonymous with contempt and amount to behaviour or language which detracts from the respect due to the authority and person of a superior.

Dissemination

The obligation to spread knowledge of international humanitarian law based on the idea that sound acquaintance of the rules set forth in the law is essential for their effective application and, consequently, for the protection of the victims of armed conflicts.

Dissolution

The process of rendering a court-martial null, abrogating or revoking it. *See* Army Act, section 117 for contingencies when a court-martial shall be dissolved.

Distinction or Discrimination, Principle of

The principle requires that combatants be distinguished from non-combatants, and that military objectives be distinguished from protected property or protected places.

Distinctive Emblem

Distinctive emblem of the red cross, red crescent or red lion and sun on a white ground used for the protection of medical units and transports, or medical and religious personnel, equipment or supplies.

[Article 8(1)—Protocol Additional to the Geneva Conventions of 12 August 1949, and relating to the Protection of Victims of International Armed Conflicts (Protocol I), 8 June, 1977.]

Distinctive Signal

Any signal or message specified for the identification exclusively of medical units or transports in Chapter III of Annex I to the Protocol referred to above.

[Article 8(m)—Protocol Additional to the Geneva Conventions of 12 August 1949, and relating to the Protection of Victims of International Armed Conflicts (Protocol I), 8 June 1977.]

Distinguished

Very successful and admired by other people, meritorious. *See* Army Rule 64.

Distribute

To deliver to the possession of another.

District Court-Martial

A type of court-martial which consists of not less than three officers which has power to try any person subject to the

Army Act other than an officer or a junior commissioned officer for any offence made punishable therein. [Army Act, sections 110, 115, 118 and 155.]

Disturbance

Actions that upset the normal state that something is in. *See* Army Act, section 59(e).

Disturbed Area

An area in which breakdown in law and order situation necessitates adoption of special security measures for the protection of life of the people as well as Government and private property. Under the Armed Forces (Special Powers) Act, 1958, the term means an area which is for the time being declared by notification under section 3 to be a disturbed area.

Doctrine of Speciality

As part of customary international law, demands that the extradited person be tried only on the charges set forth in the documentation provided in support of extradition. The doctrine is not inflexible and may be waived by the host country.

Documentary Evidence

Documentary evidence would relate to any matter expressed or described upon any substance by means of letters, figures or marks or by more than one of those means, intended to be used, or which may be used, for the purpose of recording that matter. *See* IEA, section 3.

Domicile

Place of permanent residence.

Don't Ask, Don't Tell

The policy in respect of homosexuals requires discharge of those who voluntarily declare their homosexuality, but bars military recruiters and other military personnel from inquiring into service members' sexual orientation.

Draws or Lifts Up Any Weapon Against

The phrase covers any simple assault committed in the manner stated. The drawing of any weapon in an aggressive manner or the raising or brandishing of the same in a threatening manner in the presence of and at the superior is the sort of act proscribed. The raising in a threatening manner of a firearm, whether or not loaded, of a club or of anything by which a serious blow or injury could be given is included in "lifts up".

Dual Nationality

The status of an individual with the nationality of two States.

Due Process Rights

The standard generally requires consideration of three distinct factors: the private interest that will be affected by the official action, the risk of erroneous deprivation and the value of additional or substitute procedural safeguards; and the Government's interest in the fiscal or administrative burdens.

Duel

It is combat between two persons for private reasons fought with deadly weapons with prior agreement.

Dump

A storage area, where ammunition, equipment or supplies are stocked on ground, usually in the open. *See* section 4(b) of Armed Forces (Special Powers) Act, 1958.

Duplicity

A defect in the charge wherein a single charge discloses two separate offences which makes it bad in law. *See* Notes 3 and 4 to Army Rule 30.

Duty

A duty may be imposed by treaty, statute, regulation, lawful order, standard operating procedure, or custom of the service.

Dwelling House

Is any permanent building or separate part thereof in which the owner or tenant, or any one with their consent, habitually sleeps at night.

Dwelling Unit

A single storeyed dwelling unit, duplex type unit or a flat/plot or any other type of flat/dwelling constructed in double or multi-storeyed building by the Organisation under any of the schemes. *See* AWHO Master Brochure, July 1987.

Dying Declaration

Statements made by a person since dead as to the cause of his death or any of the circumstances of the transactions which resulted in his death, irrespective of whether or not he was then under an expectation of death.

E

Efficient

Doing something well and thoroughly with no waste of time, money or energy. *See* Army Rule 13.

Elect

To choose to do something. *See* Army Act, section 84.

Elements

The essential ingredients of an offence that are to be proven at the trial.

Elements of Crime

In the context of the Rome Statute are meant to assist the court in the interpretation and application of Articles 6(genocide), 7(crimes against humanity), and 8 (war crimes).

Eligible

The term has two meanings *i.e.*, "legally qualified" or "fit to be chosen" as regards selection of persons worthy of choice.

Embargo

A prohibition on the entry or egress of shipping into a port. Nowadays, it is frequently used for prohibitions of certain categories of cargo such as munitions.

Embarrassed

Shy, awkward or ashamed, especially in a social situation. *See* Army Rules 35(4) and 79(5).

Embezzlement

Unlawful misappropriation by a servant. This offence is committed by a person employed in the capacity of clerk or servant who fraudulently misappropriates property delivered to or received or taken into possession by him for or in the name or on account of his master or employer.

Emblem

An object or a representation that functions as a symbol; a distinctive badge, design or device.

Embody

The term is used in relation to Territorial Army personnel.

Emergency

War, invasion, riot or insurrection, real or apprehended. [Section 2 of the Canada's National Defence Act, 1985.]

Emoluments

Pay and allowances, and all other items of personal remuneration drawn by an individual but do not include compensatory allowance, *e.g.*, house rent allowance. *See* Financial Regulations, Part I, section 1.

Endeavour

An attempt to do something, especially something new or difficult. *See* Army Act, section 37(e).

Endorsement

A writing on the back of a document, a public statement or action showing that you support somebody/something.

Ends of Justice

The objectives of justice. *See* Army Rule 143(4).

Enemy

The word includes all armed mutineers, armed rebels, armed rioters, poxrates and any person in arms against whom it is duty of any person subject to military law to act. *See* Army Act, section 3(x). A person subject to the Army Act, who, when a comrade 'runs amok' shows cowardice by refraining from acting against him is liable to be tried for an offence in relation to the enemy. It includes organised forces of the enemy in time of war, any hostile body that own forces may be opposing, such as a rebellious mob or a band of renegades, and includes civilians as well as members of military organisations.

Enemy Combatant

Is an individual who, under the laws and customs of war, may be detained for the duration of an armed conflict. It is a general category that subsumes two sub-categories; lawful and unlawful combatants.

Enforcement
The action of enforcing.

Enlist
Defined as to enroll on the list of a military body, to engage a soldier, to (cause to) join something especially the armed forces, enroll or enter one's name on a list especially as a commitment to membership in the armed service. To enlist comprises both the act of recruiting and the act of conscripting.

Enlistment
A basic route for induction into military service, it has characteristics of both contract and status. The typical military enlistment agreement provides for a few years of military service obligation, divided between an active duty tour and a period of reserve service.

Enroll
To place a man's name on the roll or nominal list of a body of soldiers.

Enrolling Officer
This term, as defined in Army Rule 7, relates to all Recruiting Officers, Assistant Recruiting Officers including Indian Navy or of the Air Force appointed as such, officer commanding a Regiment, Battalion, training or regimental centre and Extra Assistant Recruiting Officers, or any persons appointed as enrolling officers by the Adjutant General.

Enrolment
Is the registering or entering on the rolls of the Army. For procedure before enrolling officer, mode of enrolment and validity of enrolment etc. *see* Army Act, sections 11 to 15. Everyone who is permanently subject to military law (except officers, JCOs and WOs) is subject to that law by virtue of his 'enrolment'.

Enrolment Form
A form containing conditions of service embodied in the questions which are put by the enrolling officer to the person

desirous of being enrolled. The questions are read and explained and the person duly cautioned and his answers are recorded.

Enrolment Paper

The enrolment paper is legal evidence of the fact of enrolment and of the enrolled person having given the answers to questions which he is therein represented as having given. *See* Army Act, section 141 and Notes thereto.

Enslavement

The term means the exercise of any or all of the powers attaching to the right of ownership over a person and includes the exercise of such power in the courts of trafficking in person, in particular women and children. *See* Article 7.2(c) of the ICC Statute.

Entail

To involve something that cannot be avoided. *See* RA(DSR), para 708(a)(i).

Entitled

Having a title to. *See* Army Rule 105(1).

Entitlement

Is the recognition by the Pension Sanctioning authority after consideration of both the medical and non-medical evidence that a disability has been influenced in its onset or course by the conditions of service. Such a disability is called an "Accepted Disability". *See* Army Rule 11(1)

Entity

A person, group, trust, partnership or fund or an unincorporated association or organisation. The word includes a State or a political sub-division or agency of State.

Escape

Any completed casting off of the restraint of confinement, before release by proper authority, is an escape, and lack of effectiveness of the restraint imposed is immaterial. An escape may be either with or without force or artifice, and either with or without the consent of the custodian.

Escort

A body of troops attending an individual as a guard. The term is also applied to a guard placed over prisoners on march to prevent their escape.

Espionage

Espionage includes any clandestine action undertaken to acquire classified information by other countries, organisations or individuals for their illegitimate use. The term also includes the transmission of such information.

Essential Parameters

Minimum essential military requirements corresponding to the task or tasks to be performed by the system.

Estoppel

Doctrine according to which a subject of law is precluded from denying the truth of a statement made earlier by a duly authorised representative or the existence of a fact in which such representative has by word or conduct led others to believe.

Ethics

These concern what is right and wrong and what is moral duty and obligation. Ethics are the study of the general nature of morals and of specific moral choices. These are the rules or standards governing the conduct of members of a profession.

Evacuation

The rearward movement of equipment/personnel casualty out of an area of operations to a rear establishment for repair/ treatment.

Evidence—Direct and Indirect

By direct evidence is meant the statement of a person who saw, or otherwise observed with his senses, the fact in question. By indirect (or circumstantial) is meant evidence of facts, from which the fact in question may be inferred or presumed.

Examination-in-Chief

It is examination of a person by the party which calls him.

Examination of a Witness on Commission

When a witness is essential but cannot be called without an unreasonably extreme delay, expenses or inconvenience, the court may forward a list of questions to be put to the witness including those suggested by prosecution and defence. This must not be done in respect of a material witness. For detailed procedure see Army Act, sections 137 and 138 and notes thereto.

Exception

A person or thing that is not included in a general statement; a thing that does not follow a rule. [Army Act, section 8(2).]

Excessive

More than reasonable or necessary or unreasonably high. The term has relationship to the review of proceedings where the punishment is excessive. *See* Army Act, section 87. A punishment is excessive when it is in excess of the punishments authorised by law for the offence.

Exchange

An act of giving something to somebody or doing something for somebody and receiving something in return. *See* Army Act, section 151.

Excuse

Freedom from blame for breach of a legal rule.

Execution

The accomplishment of a thing, the completion of an act or instrument. *See* Army Act, section 169.

Execution of Office

An officer is in the execution of office when engaged in any act or service required or authorised by treaty, statute, regulation, the order of a superior, or military usage.

Exemplary Manner

A JCO, WO or OR will be considered as having served in an exemplary manner if at any time during his service subsequent to the commission of offence, he has had no red ink entry in his conduct sheet for a continuous period of three years. *See* RA(DSR), para 466(a) read with Army Act, section 122(4).

Exempt

Not subject, not liable to. Men of certain age are exempt from service in the militia. Officers on courts-martial are some times exempt from all other duties until the court is dissolved.

Exemption

A privilege to be free from certain services or appearances; or an immunity, freedom from any service charge, burden, taxes etc.

Ex-Gratia

Act of grace without acknowledgement of a legal obligation.

Exhibit

Any document or thing produced by a witness when giving his evidence shall be made an exhibit.

Exigencies

An urgent need or demand that you must deal with. *See* Army Rules 3, 81(4) and 95(2).

Existence

The state or fact of being real or living, a way of living especially when this is difficult or boring. *See* Army Act, section 37(d).

Existing Explosive Remnants of War

Unexploded ordnance and abandoned explosive ordnance that existed prior to the entry into force of the Protocol V to the 1980 Convention for the High Contracting Party on whose territory it exists.

See Article 2.5 of Protocol on Explosive Remnants of War (Protocol V to the 1980 Convention).

Existing Scale

The term in relation to an officer means integrated pay scale or fixed rate of pay of the rank applicable to him as on 01 January, 1996 whether held in a substantive or acting capacity. *See* Army Instructions 2/S/1998.

Ex Parte

Of the one part; from one party. This term is applied in law to a proceeding by one party in the absence of, and without notice to, the other. RA(DSR), para 538.

Expatriation

(1) Voluntary: Renunciation of nationality by an individual.
(2) Compulsory: Deprivation of nationality by act of State.

Explanation

A reason given for something, a statement, fact or situation that tells you why something happened. *See* Army Rule 15.

Explosive Ordnance

Conventional munitions containing explosives, with the exception of mines, booby traps and other devices as defined in Protocol II.

See Article 2.1 of Protocol on Explosive Remnants of War (Protocol V to the 1980 Convention).

Explosive Remnants of War

Unexploded ordnance and abandoned explosive ordnance. *See* Article 2.4 of Protocol on Explosive Remnants of War (Protocol V to the 1980 Convention).

Expression

A word or phrase, opinions and ideas, a look on a person's face that shows their thoughts or feelings. *See* Army Act, section 2(xxv).

Extension

Enlarging, or giving further duration to, the continuance of an existing thing.

Extension of Service

A soldier extending his period of army service instead of going to the Reserve in accordance with the terms of his original enlistment, or extending the term of his original enlistment to a given number of years, or any shorter period.

Extermination

The term includes intentional infliction of conditions of life, *inter alia* deprivation of access to food and medicine, calculated to bring about the destruction of part of a population. *See* Article 7.2 (b) of the ICC Statute.

Extortion

The action or practice of wresting anything, especially money, from a person by force or by undue exercise of authority or power; an act of illegal exaction. *See* Army Act, section 53.

Extradition

Delivering up of a suspected or convicted person by one State to another as provided by treaty, convention or national legislation. *See* Article 102 of the Rome Statute.

Extra Guards

One of the punishments indicated in Army Act, section 80.

Extra-Judicial Executions

These are unlawful and deliberate killings carried out by order of a Government or with its complicity or acquiescence.

Extra-Regimental Employment

Employment on military duties other than staff (including Corps Staff) or Regimental employment on secondment. *See* RA(DSR) – explanation of terms used.

Extra-Territoriality

Exemption from local jurisdiction.

F

Facility

Services, building, equipment etc. that are provided for a particular purpose. *See* Army Rule 36.

Failed State

A failed State is one in which the Government does not have effective control over its territory, is not perceived as legitimate by a significant portion of its population, does not provide security or basic public services to its citizens, and lacks a monopoly on the use of force.

Fair and Regular Trial

Elements required, under war crime context, to ensure a fair and regular trial, include, but are not limited to, the following:—

- the right to counsel.
- the right to prepare a defence (including the right to present witnesses and evidence).
- the right to be informed of the charges against the accused.

- the right to have a judgment rendered by an independent and impartial court.
- the right to an interpreter.
- the length of the trial may be considered in evaluating the fairness of the proceedings (for example, a very short trial may indicate that the accused did not have sufficient time to prepare an adequate defence).

False

Erroneous, untrue. The term does not necessarily involve turpitude of mind.

False Accusation

It implies an accusation (verbal or written) made to some superior authority which would lead to the latter exercising his authority by inquiry or otherwise, or some assertion made publicly or to another person which if true would expose the person (respecting whom it is made) to punishment or moral censure. *See* Note 2 to Army Act, section 56.

False Alarm

Spreading of false or disturbing rumours or reports, as well as the false giving of established alarm signals. *See* Army Act, section 34(g).

False Document

A document is false if it or any material part of it purports to be made by or on behalf of a person who did not make it or authorise its making, and in particular, if any material alteration by addition, insertion or obliteration has been made in it, or if the whole or some material part of it purports to have been made by or on behalf of a fictitious or deceased person.

Family

The Government Servant's wife (one wife only) or husband, as the case may be, parents, sisters, minor brother, legitimate/ legally adopted children (including widowed sisters, provided their father is either not alive or is himself wholly dependent on the Government servant concerned, major sons, married/widowed daughters) step children and step-mother residing with and wholly dependent on him/her. However, for the purpose of journeys to and from abroad and from one station to another station abroad, the term 'family' will not include parents, sisters and minor brothers. [Travel Regulations, para 2.]

Fatigue

The term given to a party of soldiers told off for any other duty than a dress necessitates.

Feasible Precautions

Are those precautions which are practicable or practically possible taking into account all circumstances ruling at the time, including humanitarian and military considerations.

Article 1(5) Protocol on Prohibitions or Restrictions on the Use of Incendiary Weapons (Protocol III), Geneva, 10 October 1980.

Feign

To feign disease or infirmity means that the accused person exhibits appearances resembling the genuine symptoms of disease or infirmity, which to his knowledge, are not due to such disease or infirmity, but have been produced artificially for purpose of deceit *e.g.*, simulating fits or mental disease. *See* Note 8 to Army Act, section 46.

Feres Doctrine

Or "incident to service rule" is based primarily on the peculiar and special relationship of the soldier to his superiors and adverse effects of maintenance of tort suits on discipline. To allow suits against superior officers would disrupt military discipline. [*Feres* v. *United States* (S.Ct. 1950).]

Fiduciary

A person holding a special relationship of trust, confidence, or duty to act primarily for another's benefit. *See* RA(DSR), para 807.

Field Area

An area where troops are deployed near the borders or in the hinterland for operational requirements and where imminence of hostilities/violence and associated risk to life exists. Such areas lack infrastructural facilities and troops are located for reasons of operational considerations alone and remain heavily committed in security related duties.

Field Conduct Sheets

These are prepared in peace for all serving soldiers and reservists.

Field Officer

The term includes an officer not being a general officer of any rank (including brevet rank) above the rank of Captain. *See* Army Rule 2(c).

Field Punishment

These punishments were awardable on conviction by a court-martial to a person under the rank of a WO committing any offence on active service.

Fighters

A specific group which as such takes part in hostilities in an organised form and may always be the object of attacks. The essential difference between fighters and unprotected civilians is, however, that the latter regain their protected status if they cease to take a direct part in hostilities, while fighters remain subject to individualised attacks even if they cease fighting (unless they become a person *hors de combat*).

Final Address

After the end of the case for prosecution and where the accused does not call witness, the address made by a prosecutor is called final address. *See* Army Rule 58(c).

Finance Cost

Finance cost is the additional cost charged to the allottee to bring parity between registrants or/and to offset interest burden carried by the organization. *See* AWHO Master Brochure, July 1987.

Finding

The decision or the verdict of the court is its finding on every charge upon which an accused is arraigned. It is recorded simply as a finding of "Guilty" or "Not Guilty". *See* Army Rules 61 and 62.

Finding of Insanity

This finding is recorded where the court finds either that the accused by reason of unsoundness of mind is incapable of making his defence, or that he committed the act alleged but was, by reason of unsoundness of mind incapable of knowing the nature of the act or that it was wrong or contrary to law. *See* Army Rule 145.

Fine

A pecuniary punishment for an offence. *See* RA(DSR), para 532.

Fire-arm

Any portable weapon that expels, is designed to expel or may be readily converted to expel a shot bullet, or projectile by the action of an explosive, excluding antique fire-arms and their replicas shall be defined in accordance with domestic law. In no case, however, shall antique fire-arms include fire-arms manufactured after 1899. [Article 3(a) of the Protocol against the Illicit Manufacturing of and Trafficking in Fire-arms, their Parts and Components and Ammunition, supplementing the United Nations Convention against Transnational Organised Crime.]

Fit

To agree with, match or be suitable for something or for a particular job; suitable, of the right quality. *See* Army Rule 8.

Flag of Truce

White flag indicating desire for peace. *See* Army Act, section 34(f) and 35(c).

Flag Officers

Admirals who hoist flags at the mast heads. Vide section 3(8) of the Navy Act, it means an officer of the rank of Admiral of the Fleet, Admiral, Vice-Admiral or Rear-Admiral.

Flag Ship

Ship with admiral on board.

Flogging

A barbarous punishment formerly inflicted in the British Army and Navy. It was generally inflicted with a whip, or "cat of nine tails" on the bare back.

Followers

The settlers, traders and dealers generally; also civilian employees, servants, and women who follow troops, and are amenable to the regulations and restrictions of the service. *See* Army Act, section 2(1)(l).

Force

An aggregation of military personnel, weapon systems, vehicles and necessary support, or combination thereof.

Forces

The Army, Navy and Air Force, or any part of any one or more of them. *See* Army Act, section 3(xi) and section 2(xii-b) of the Cantonment Act, 1924. For the purpose of Army Act, section 36(a), when used as a verb will include passing the sentry when warned by him not to do so.

Force Abandonment

Actions resulting from a decision approved by the Force Commander or his authorised representative that results in the loss of custody and control of equipment and supplies.

Force Commander

In the context of a UN Peace keeping Mission means the officers appointed under the authority of the Secretary General, responsible for all military operations within the mission.

Force Majeure

Event beyond human control.

Forced Pregnancy

The unlawful confinement of a woman forcibly made pregnant with the intent of affecting the ethnic composition of any population or carrying out other grave violations of international law. This definition shall not in any way be interpreted as affecting national laws relating to pregnancy. *See* Article 2.1(f) of the ICC Statute.

Forcibly

The term is not restricted to physical force, but may include threat of force or coercion, such as that caused by fear of violence, duress, detention, psychological oppression or abuse of power against such person or persons or another person, or by taking advantage of a coercive environment.

Forcing a Safeguard

To perform an act or acts in violation of the protection of the safeguard.

Foreign Intelligence

Information or intelligence about the capabilities, intentions or activities of a foreign individual State, organisation or terrorist group, as they relate to international affairs, defence or security. [Section 273.61 of Canada's National Defence Act, 1985.]

Foreign State

Under the Constitution of India, the term means any State other than India. *See* Article 367(3).

Forfeit

To render oneself by misdeeds liable to be deprived of; as, a soldier forfeits pay by sentence of court-martial for offences committed.

Forfeiture

The act of forfeiting something. It is the act of loosing something or to have something taken away because one has done something wrong.

Forgery

Making of a false document in order that it may be used as genuine with intent to defraud.

Form D

Refers to a military certificate form of concession voucher meant for officers when travelling on leave at their own expense and for their families.

Formal Investigation

Before a charge may be referred to a court-martial for trial, a formal investigation is required. This investigation has two purposes. First, it screens charges prior to trial by a court-martial, impartially weighing the facts to determine whether the case should be brought to trial. Second, it provides the defence with some discovery and gives an opportunity for an early exoneration from charges.

Forthwith

Immediately, as soon as by reasonable exertion, or without delay.

Fraudulent Conversion

The offence is committed by every person who—(i) being entrusted either solely or jointly with any other person with any property in order that he may retain in safe custody or apply, pay or deliver, for any purpose or to any person, the property or any part thereof, or (ii) having either solely or jointly with any other person received any property for or on account of any other person, fraudulently converts to his use or benefit, or the use or benefit of any other person, the property or any part thereof or any proceeds thereof.

Fraudulent Enrolment

When a person absents himself from one Corps and re-enrols himself in the same or another Corps, or enrolls himself in the Navy, Air Force or TA. *See* Notes 5 and 6 to Army Act, section 43.

Freedom of the Seas

Exclusive jurisdiction of flag-State over ships on the high seas in time of peace. Limited in time of war.

Friend of the Accused

He is a person who assists the accused at his trial by any court-martial. He may be of any rank, or he may be a civilian. He may or may not be legally qualified.

Frontier Post

Military posts deployed in that part of country which fronts or faces another country; hence a fortified or guarded position.

Fugitive

A person who has escaped or is running away from somewhere and is trying to avoid being caught.

Full Pay

The pecuniary allowance which was made to officers and non-commissioned officers, without any deduction whatsoever.

Functional Interpretation

Interpretation of a document in accordance with its purpose.

Functions

Employment, discharge of office, the kind of action proper to a person as belonging to a class. *See* Army Act, section 3(v).

Funds

Funds mean assets of every kind, whether tangible or intangible, movable or immovable, however acquired, and legal documents or instruments in any form including electronic or digital, evidencing title to, or interest in, such assets, including, but not limited to, bank credits, travellers cheques, bank cheque, money orders, shares, securities, bonds, drafts and letters of credit. *See* Article 3 to Additional Protocol to the SAARC Regional Convention on Suppression of Terrorism, Islamabad, 6 Jan 2004. Also *see* RA(DSR), para 801.

Furlough

Leave of absence granted to officers and soldiers of the Army; authorised absence from duty granted to an enlisted man by his commanding officer.

G

Gallantry Award

Award for courage, especially in a battle.

Garrison

Troops stationed in fortress, town etc. to defend it. A place in which troops are quartered.

Gated

A form of non-judicial punishment usually common in military academies, when a cadet is not allowed to go beyond the area specified.

General Court-Martial

A court-martial which may impose death sentence, dishonourable discharge and dismissal and, in general, any punishment not specifically barred by the military law.

General, Local or Other Order

In the context of Army Act, section 39(f), would mean standing order or orders in writing and applicable continuously over a period of time to persons present in certain geographical area, or in a particular formation.

General Officers

All officers whose authority extends beyond the immediate command of a regiment, and who have either separate districts or departments at home, or commands on foreign service.

General Orders

Are orders that are issued to announce the hours for roll calls and duties; the number and kind of orderlies and the time when they shall be relieved; police regulations, and the prohibitions required by circumstances and localities; returns to be made and their forms; laws and regulations for the army; promotions and appointments; eulogies or censures to corps or individuals, and generally whatever may be important to make known to the whole command.

Generality

Total applicability. *See* Army Act, section 191(2).

Geneva Conventions

The four Geneva Conventions of 12 August, 1949, constitute the body of rules of protection to safeguard the victims of situations of armed conflict – members of the armed forces who are out of action, as well as the civilian population and generally all persons not or no longer taking part in hostilities.

Geneva Type Law

It deals with the protection of war victims, be they military or civilians, on land or on water. It protects all persons *hors de combat i.e.,* not or no longer taking part in hostilities: the wounded, the sick, the ship-wrecked and POWs.

Genocide

One of the most serious crimes of concern to the international community as a whole and involving acts enumerated in Article 6 to the ICC Statute. Such acts must be committed with intent to destroy, in whole or in part, a national, ethnical, racial or religious group.

Gift

Defined as any gratuity, favour, discount, entertainment, hospitality, loan, forbearance, or other item having monetary value. It includes service as well as gifts of training, transportation, local travel, lodging and meals, whether provided in kind, by purchase of a ticket, payment in advance, or reimbursement after the expense has been incurred.

Global Information Infrastructure

Includes electro-magnetic emissions, communication systems, information technology systems and networks, and any data or technical information carried on, contained in or relating to those emissions, systems or networks. Section 273.61 of Canada's National Defence Act, 1985.

Good Behaviour

The term has been used in the context of order to give security for good behaviour under the Code of Criminal Procedure. *See* Rule 4(i) of the Territorial Army Act Rules, 1948.

Good Faith

Nothing is said to be done or believed in good faith which is done or believed without due care and attention. *See* IPC, section 52. Also means exercise of legal rights in accordance with moral minimum standards received into international law.

Good Offices

Endeavour by a third State to bring together States in disputes and to induce them to settle the question at issue.

Good Order

The words 'good order' as used in Army Act, section 63, are wide enough to include good order in the sense in which the words would be understood in civil life and applicable to civilians, and in the sense in which they would they would be understood in military life as applicable to members of a military force. Conduct which is to the prejudice of good order is not necessarily to the prejudice of military discipline. On the other hand, conduct which is prejudicial to military discipline is also prejudicial to good order in the military sense, as applicable to members of a military force.

Grade

A step or degree, in a graduated scale of office or military rank that is established and designated as a grade by law or regulation.

Graded Staff Appointment

Appointments dealing with Army matters in general and tenable by officers of all Arms and Services. *See* RA(DSR) – explanation of terms used.

Grammatical Interpretation

Interpretation of a document in accordance with the syntax of words.

Gratification

Certain rewards which generals gave to the troops, after a severe engagement, in testimony of their valour and good conduct. These rewards were distributed according to rank.

Gratuity

An allowance granted for the purpose of augmenting an officer's emoluments without giving him a claim to a higher rate of net terminal benefits.

Grave Breaches

These are abuses and infractions of the law of war as enumerated in the Geneva Conventions and which attract effective penal sanctions. These represent some of the most serious violations of international humanitarian law. They are specific acts listed in the Geneva Conventions and Protocol I including wilful killing, torture or in-human treatment and willfully causing great injury. Grave breaches are regarded as war crimes.

Group

A unit of the Security Guard constituted as a group by the Central Government. *See* section 2(1)(j) of the NSG Act, 1986.

Group Ethics

The set of beliefs about right and wrong, good and bad, morals and duties that originate from a group of individuals.

Group Rights

Additional rights accruing to individuals by virtue of their being members of a particular group or class of individuals, *e.g.*, senior citizens rights.

"Guilty" Plea

It admits every element of the crime specified and if accepted is equivalent to a conviction.

H

Hague Type Law

Is concerned with regulation of the methods and means of combat and concentrates on the conduct of military operations.

Half Pay

A compensation or retaining fee which was given to officers who had retired from the service through age, inability etc. or who had been placed upon that list in consequence of a general reduction of the forces or a partial drafting etc. of the particular corps to which they belonged. The half pay became due on 25th of June, and on the 25th of December in each year but was seldom issued until three months after expiration of each of these periods.

Harbour

An area where a force lies up for any length of time to refit, rest, reorganise and to be maintained.

Harbouring

The word 'harbour' include supplying a person with shelter, food, drinks, money, clothes, arms, ammunition or means of conveyance or the assisting of a person by any means, whether of the above kind or to evade apprehension. *See* Note 19 to Army Act, section 34.

Hard Core of Human Rights

Include the right to life and prohibition of torture and other cruel, inhuman or degrading treatment or punishment.

Hardship Exemption

In the context of entry into the military means, exemption granted to prevent substantial harm to persons dependant on the registrant.

Hazard

A rare or extreme natural or human made event that threatens to adversely affect human life, property or activity to the extent of causing disaster.

Hazardous Duty or Important Service

These may include service such as duty in combat or other dangerous area; embarkation for certain foreign or sea duty; movement to a port of embarkation for that purpose; entrainment for duty on the border or coast in time of war or threatened invasion or other disturbances; strike or riot duty; or employment in aid to civil power in, for example, protecting property, or quelling or preventing disorder in times of great public disaster. Whether a duty in hazardous or a service is important depends upon the circumstances of the particular case; and is a question of fact for the court-martial to decide. *See* US MCM IV-12.

Head of Mission

The Special Representative appointed by the Secretary-General with the consent of the Security Council responsible for all United Nations activities within the mission.

Headquarter

The administration and tactical office of an organisation consisting of the commanding officer, his staff, and the necessary personnel for administrative and tactical activities; the residence of the commander-in-chief, whether in camp or elsewhere.

Hide

A place of concealment which is previously re-connoitred and where a unit, sub-unit or its components may be required to wait for orders prior to executive action.

Hearing of Charge

This is the first stage in the investigation of charges. Every charge against a person subject to the Army Act shall be heard by the Commanding Officer in the presence of accused. The accused shall have full liberty to cross-examine any witness against him, and to call such witness and make such statement as may be necessary for his defence. *See* Army Rule 22.

Hearsay Evidence

It is what a person does not say of his own knowledge but what another has said or signified to him. It may be oral or written. It is the oral or written statement of a person who is not produced in Court, conveyed to the Court either by a witness or the instrumentality of a document. As a rule, such evidence is not admissible as the statements are not made on oath or affirmation, and the person affected had no opportunity of cross examining their author.

Hegemony

The position of factual pre-imminence in the relations between sovereign and equal States.

High Seas

The water on the seaward side of the territorial sea.

Hinterland

Interior of a sea coast.

Holy Wars

These are understood to be wars of aggression waged with a claimed missionizing purpose at the command of a given divinity.

Homosexual Acts

These are defined to include any bodily contact, actively undertaken or passively permitted, between members of the same sex for the purpose of satisfying sexual desires or any such contact which a reasonable person would understand to be for such a purpose.

Honour, Court of

Is a species of board of inquiry, which has not only the power of ascertaining the degree of guilt which may be attached to misconduct, but of pronouncing an opinion which may or may not entail ignominy upon the guilty persons.

Honours of War

A compliment granted on capitulation to a garrison which has made a gallant defense.

Hors de Combat

A person is *'hors de combat'* if:—

(a) he is in the power of an adverse party,

(b) he clearly expresses an intention to surrender, or

(c) he has been rendered unconscious or is otherwise incapacitated by wounds or sickness, and therefore is incapable of defending himself:

Provided that in any of these cases he abstains from any hostile act and does not attempt to escape. [Article 41(1) and (2) AP I read with Article 23(c) of 1907 Hague Regs.]

Hostages

Any persons given in pledge for the performance of conditions.

Hostile

(a) A track classification based upon established criteria, indicating the airborne object to be that of an enemy.

(b) An armed person who generally operates clandestinely belonging to a group/body of people whose activities are concerned with resistance to lawfully constituted Government and the security forces. Such groups/body of people have been declared unlawful organisation by an act of Parliament. Also means strongly rejecting or opposed to something. *See* RA(DSR), para 602(d).

Hostile Act

An attack or other use of force against the country, forces, and in certain circumstances, nationals, their property, commercial assets, and/or other designated non-own country forces, foreign nationals and their property. It is also force used directly to preclude or impede the mission and/or duties of own-forces including the recovery of own personnel and vital own-Government property. A hostile act triggers the right to use proportional force in self defence to deter, neutralise or destroy the threat. Hostile act and harmful act describe acts which terminate the special protection against direct attack afforded to persons other than civilians, namely medical, religious and civil defence personnel of the armed forces and combatants *hors de combat*.

Hostile Action

An incident from the action(s) of one or more belligerents, which has a direct and significant negative impact on the personnel and/or equipment of a troop-contributing country. Different activities may be characterised as a single hostile action when these activities can be related to each other on common ground.

Hostile Force

Any civilian, para military, or military force or terrorist(s), with or without national designation, that has committed a hostile act, exhibited hostile intent, or has been declared hostile by appropriate authority of the own Government.

Hostile Intent

The threat of imminent use of force against the own country, forces or other designated persons and property. It is also the threat of force used directly to preclude or impede the mission and/or duties of own forces, including the recovery of own personnel and vital Government property. When hostile intent is present, the right exists to use proportional force in self defence to deter, neutralise or destroy the threat. It is intended as an action which, on the basis of concrete facts, is seen as a probable and imminent threat, on the part of individuals, groups or units to cause damage to the forces being employed there or to the territorial entity they are protecting.

Hostile Witness

A witness who appears to be directly hostile to the party calling him, or unwilling to give evidence. He may with the permission of the court be treated as hostile *i.e.*, as if he were called by the other party. The calling party may ask him leading questions, cross examine him, ask him questions which tend to show his bad character and impeach his character. *See* IEA, section 154.

Hostilities

The notion is used to designate defensive or offensive acts and military operations carried out by a belligerent during an armed conflict. The term encompasses a state of enmity between individuals or nations, an act or series of acts displaying antagonism. Used in the singular, this term is not limited to an armed conflict situation, and therefore, seems to have a much broader sense than the plural 'hostilities'. Hostilities included preparations for and return from combat. The word covers not only the time that a combatant actually makes use of a weapon but also, for example, the time that he is carrying it as well as situations which he undertakes hostile acts without using a weapon. These are acts that directly cause harmful consequences to the adversary. It means the application of force or otherwise disadvantaging the opponents militarily, including intelligence activities. These comprise a wider variety of measures than just the infliction of harm on enemy personnel or property. These activities are directed at injuring or neutralizing the personnel or equipment of the adversary in the context of an armed conflict.

Hot Pursuit

The right of a littoral State to pursue into the high seas a foreign merchant ship which has committed an offence against its municipal law inside its internal waters, territorial sea or possibly, in the contiguous zone adjoining its territorial sea.

Human Rights

Legal entitlements which every person, as a human being, possesses. They are universal and belong to everyone, rich or poor, male or female. Such rights may be violated but they can never be taken away. Human rights are inherent entitlements which belong to every person as a consequence of being human.

Human Smuggling

The importation of people into a country involving deliberate evasion of immigration laws. This offence includes bringing illegal aliens as well as the unlawful transportation and harbouring of aliens already in the country concerned.

Human Trafficking

Sex trafficking in which a commercial sex act is induced by force, fraud or coercion, or in which the person induced to perform such act has not attained 18 years of age; or the recruitment harbouring, transportation, provision or obtaining of a person for labour or services, through the use of force, fraud or coercion for the purpose of subjection to involuntary servitude, peonage, debt bondage or slavery.

Humanity, Principle of

The principle of humanity or unnecessary suffering calls for minimise unnecessary suffering, incidental injury to people and collateral damage to property. As one of the fundamental principles of humanitarian law, it is born of a desire to prevent and alleviate human suffering wherever it may be found. Its purpose is to protect life and health and to ensure respect for human beings. It promotes mutual understanding, friendship, cooperation and lasting peace amongst all people.

Hut

Any building, no material portion of which above the plint level is constructed of masonary or of squared timber framing or of iron framing. *See* section 2(xvi) of the Cantonment Act, 1924.

I

Identification

Proof in a legal proceeding that a person, document, or other thing is that which it is alleged to be.

Identification Parade

A parade conducted in order to test if a witness is able to identify the accused. *See* RA(DSR), para 406.

Ill Treating

To treat somebody in a cruel or unkind way. Ill treatment of a subordinate is one of the military offences punishable under the code.

Illegal

The words illegal means contrary to law and is applicable to everything which is an offence or which is prohibited by law. An order is illegal if it is opposed to any enactment or any rule having the force of law. The word has the same meaning as 'unlawful'.

In relation to a sentence, this would mean a punishment which is prohibited by law. It will also be illegal if it is opposed to any enactment or any Rule having the force of law. For example, a sentence of imprisonment awarded by a DCM to a WO or a sentence of reduction awarded to a Lance Naik. *See* Note 2 to Army Rule 73.

Illegal Act

Act or omission amounting to breach of a legal obligation.

Illegal Award

The reduction of a Warrant Officer or a non-commissioned officer from or to an acting rank or an appointment is an example of an illegal award. *See* RA(DSR), para 469.

Illegal Omissions

An omission to do what a person is legally bound to do. Where the law imposes upon a person the duty of performing some particular act he is held responsible, if he omits to do so.

Illicit Manufacturing

In the context of fire-arms means the manufacturing or assembly of fire-arm, their parts and components or ammunition:—

(i) from parts and components illicitly trafficked.

(ii) without a licence or authorisation from a competent authority of the State Party where the manufacture or assembly takes place, or

(iii) without marking the fire-arms at the time of manufacture, in accordance with Article 8 of the Protocol noted below.

Licensing or authorisation of the manufacture of parts and components shall be in accordance with domestic law. [Article 3(d) of the Protocol against the Illicit Manufacturing of and Trafficking in Fire-arms, their Parts and Components and Ammunition, supplementing the United Nations Convention against Transnational Organised Crime.]

Illicit Trafficking

In the context of fire-arms means the import, export, acquisition, sale, delivery, movements or transfer of fire-arms, their parts and components and ammunition from or across the territory of one State Party to that of another. [Article 3(e) of the Protocol against the Illicit Manufacturing of and Trafficking in Fire-arms, their Parts and Components and Ammunition, supplementing the United Nations Convention against Transnational Organised Crime.]

Immunity

A personal favour granted by law contrary to general rule; an exemption from some general duty or burden, *e.g.*, immunity from attachment (Army Act, section 28); immunity from arrest for debt (Army Act, section 29) or immunity of persons attending court-martial from arrest (Army Act, section 30).

Impartial

Not partial, not favouring one party more than another; unprejudiced, disinterested, equitable, just. *See* Army Rules 90 and 105(8).

Impartiality

The word 'impartial' means not supporting one person or group more than another; neutral, unbiased. The principle is centred on providing assistance to people rather than to States or rebel movements and forces an organisation to avoid thinking of groups of people as 'good' or 'bad' victims.

Impediment

Disability or hindrance or obstacle etc. *See* Army Act, section 14.

Imperfect War

War that falls short of accepted international definition of war.

Imperil

To put something/somebody in danger. *See* Army Act, section 34(l).

Implementation

The term covers all measures that must be taken to ensure that the rules of international humanitarian law are fully respected.

Impliedly

Implicity, by implication. *See* Army Rule 32(2).

Impose

To introduce a new law, rule, tax etc. To force somebody/ something to have to deal with something that is difficult or unpleasant. *See* Army Act, section 89(1).

Impoundment

Any executive action to withhold or delay spending appropriated funds as intended by the Parliament. There are two funds of impoundments; deferrals and rescissions.

Impracticable

It is defined as incapable of being effected from lack of adequate means; impossible of performance; not feasible. Impossible in practise to do or carry out. In more general senses, often to mean 'unrealistic' or 'not sensible'. May sometimes be synonymous with 'impossible'. The word means not practicable, incapable of being performed or accomplished by the means employed or at command. See *UOI* v. *Harjeet Singh Sandhu,* Mil LJ 2001 SC 12.

Imprest

Cash assignment in the nature of a permanent advance placed at the disposal of officers incurring expenditure such as local purchase of petty stores, local repairs by civilian firms, contingent or postal charges and payments for casual labour on daily rates of pay, paid through muster rolls, which is accounted for in contingent bills and reimbursed once a month or more frequently, if desired. Financial Regulations Vol I, Part 1, section 1, RA(DSR), para 802(b).

Impressment

The term is usually used for compulsory hiring of civil mechanical transport or carriages; with the horses (or other animals) for the movement of troops on mobilization.

Imprisoned Person

Any person deprived of personal liberty as a result of conviction for an offence.

Imprudence

Want of being wise or sensible, unwise. *See* Army Act, section 91(d) and RA(DSR), para 1228.

In Camera

In chamber, in private (as opposed to 'in open court').

In Lieu of

In place of, instead. *See* RA(DSR), para 817(c).

Incapable

Wanting in capacity or ability. A term of disgrace, frequently annexed to military sentences, when an officer has been cashiered by the sentence of a court-martial and rendered incapable of ever serving his country in either a civil or military capacity.

Incapacitated

Unfit or unable to perform properly.

Incendiary Weapon

Any weapon or munition:

(a) Which is primarily designed to set fire to objects or to cause burn injury to persons through the action of flame, heat, or combination thereof, produced by use of incendiary substances.

(b) Incendiary weapons do not include:

  (i) Munitions which may have incidental incendiary effects, such as illuminants, tracers, smoke or signalling systems;

  (ii) Munitions designed to combine penetration, blast or fragmentation effects with an additional incendiary effect, such as armour-piercing projectiles, fragmentation shells, explosive bombs and similar combined-effects munitions in which the incendiary effect is not specifically designed to cause burn injury to persons, but to be used against military objectives, such as armoured vehicles, aircraft and installations or facilities.

See Article 1(1) Protocol on Prohibitions or Restrictions on the Use of Incendiary Weapons (Protocol III), Geneva, 10 October 1980.

Inchoate Proceeding

Imperfect, incomplete or unfinished proceedings.

Incidence

A happening, an act or the fact or manner of falling upon or affecting. *See* Army Act, section 191(2)(b).

Incident to Service Test

In the context of claim for military malpractices means, that the focus is not on where the treatment was rendered or by whom, but rather on the service member's military status in relation to the treatment.

Incidental Question

It is one which may refer to any point of law, evidence or procedure, *e.g.*, as to admissibility of evidence, propriety of any question to a witness, recalling of a witness. It may be raised by prosecutor or accused, opposite party has a right to answer and the party raising it has a right of reply. *See* Army Rule 88.

Incite

To encourage somebody to do something violent, illegal or unpleasant, especially by making them angry or excited. *See* Army Act, section 37(a).

Incumbent

A person who has an official position. *See* RA(DSR), para 811.

Incursion

Invasion without conquest; inroad or ravage.

Indecency

An act against good behaviour and just delicacy. Indecent means that which is offensive to modesty. Not decent, unfit to be heard or seen.

Indemnify

To make good a loss which one person has suffered in consequence of the act or default of another. *See* RA(DSR), para 1395.

Indemnity

Compensation or remuneration for loss, damage or injury sustained.

Indent

An official order for goods or equipment. *See* RA(DSR), para 813.

Indian Navy

The regular naval forces raised and maintained by the Central Government. *See* Navy Act, section 3(10).

Indian Naval Reserve Force

The Naval Reserve Forces raised and maintained by the Central Government. *See* Navy Act, section 3(9).

Indian Waters

The seas extending from the shores of India to such limits as may be prescribed. *See* Navy Act, section 3(11).

Indisciplinable

Not disciplinable, incapable of being disciplined, or subjected to discipline, undisciplinable.

Indiscipline

Want of discipline or instruction.

Indiscriminate Attacks

Are:

(a) those which are not directed at a specific military objective;

(b) those which employ a method or means of combat which cannot be directed at a specific military objective; or

(c) Those which employ a method or means of combat the effects of which cannot be limited as required by this Protocol;

and consequently, in each such case, are of a nature to strike military objectives and civilians or civilian objects without distinction. Among others, the following types of attacks are to be considered as indiscriminate:

(a) an attack by bombardment by any methods or means which treats as a single military objective a number of clearly separated and distinct military objectives located in a city, town, village or other area containing a similar concentration of civilians or civilian objectives; and

(b) an attack which may be expected to cause incidental loss of civilian life, injury to civilians, damage to civilian objects, or a combination thereof, which would be excessive in relation to the concrete and direct military advantage anticipated.

Article 51(4) and (5)—Protocol Additional to the Geneva Conventions of 12 August 1949, and relating to the Protection of Victims of International Armed Conflicts (Protocol I), 8 June 1977.

Individual Criminal Responsibility

For some international crimes, individual may be held criminally liable before international or national tribunals—war crimes are a classic case.

Induce

To persuade or influence somebody to do something. *See* Army Act, section 34(a).

Indulgence

The state or act of having or doing whatever you want, the state of allowing somebody to have or do whatever they want. *See* Army Act, section 64(e).

Industry

The people and activities involved in producing a particular thing, or in providing a particular service. *See* Army Act, section 177(c).

Inefficiency

Not eligible, not doing a job well. *See* Army Rule 15.

Inefficient

Incapable of, or indisposed to effective action, effecting nothing.

Ineligibility

The term is used with reference to the disability or legal incapacity of an officer to serve as a member of a court-martial. *See* Army Rule 39(1).

Inexpedient

Of an action, not fair or right. *See* Army Act, section 117(3).

Inexperienced

Not having experience, unskilled.

Infamous Behaviour

In the British service a term peculiarly applicable to military life when it is effected by dishonorable conduct; on conviction of which an officer is ordered to be cashiered. For example, it has always been deemed infamous and disgraceful to abandon the field of action or to desert the colours.

Inferior

Not good or not as good as somebody/something else; of lower rank. *See* Army Act, sections 6, 7 and 42.

Infirmity

An imperfection or weakness, especially a disease. *See* Army Act, section 46(b).

Informally Expressed

A punishment would be informally expressed when it is not recorded in the manner indicated, *e.g.*, a term of rigorous imprisonment for twenty four months would be said to be informally expressed as it is required to be recorded as two years.

Information

Any and every piece of evidence and data, which may be relevant or irrelevant, true or false, in its raw and unprocessed form.

Inhabitant

In relation to a cantonment, or local area means any person ordinarily residing or carrying on business or owning or occupying immovable property therein, and in case of a dispute means any person declared by the District Magistrate to be an inhabitant; *See* section 2(xviii) of the Cantonment Act, 1924 and Army Act, section 64(f).

Inhuman Treatment

Is an intentional act or omission, which judged objectively, is deliberate and not accidental, which causes serious mental or physical suffering or injury or constitutes a serious attack on human dignity. During the ICTY Judgment in *The Prosecutor* v. *Zejnil Delalic and Others*, IT-96-21-T, para 543, the ICTY Prosecution defined the mental elements of this crime as follows:

The accused or his subordinate(s) intended to unlawfully impair the physical, intellectual or moral integrity of the protected person or otherwise subject him or her to indignities, pain, suffering out of proportion to the treatment expected of one human being to another.

Injunction

Authoritative order or judicial process restraining a person from wrongful act. *See* Army Act, section 123(2).

Innocent Passage

Rights of foreign ships to traverse territorial waters.

Inoperative

In relation to a punishment will denote a sentence when the existence of the law is recognised but its operation is stopped during the time or the one that is without practical force, *e.g.*, a sentence reducing a Naik/acting Havildar to Naik or Lance Naik, or a Lance Naik to the ranks is inoperative. The statute does not debar reduction from an acting rank. It is only a guideline as indicated in Note 10(b) to section 71 which shows that a court-martial does not deal with acting rank.

Inquiry

Is the aiming at or discovery of truth by question, either formal, verbal interrogation, or a recourse to the proper means and sources of knowledge when the object has been shaped into a question or problem for solution.

Insignia

Any characteristic marks, distinguished signs or badges of office or honour worn on uniforms of members of the armed services to indicate their branch of service, rank or grade, organisation etc.

Inspect

View closely and critically, to examine, to investigate or oversee officially. *See* Army Rules 93 and 97(3).

Inspector

A person whose job is to visit. *See* Army Act, section 177(b).

Institution

Large important organization that has a particular purpose or a building where people with special needs are taken care of. *See* Army Act, sections 52 & 55(a).

Insubordinate Language

The use of words, which either in themselves, or in the manner or circumstances in which they are spoken, be insulting or disrespectful or indicating intention to resist lawful authority. It must reasonably appear that they were intended to be heard by a superior. *See* Notes 9, 11 and 15 to Army Act, sections 40 and 42.

Insubordination

Refusal to subordinate oneself to authority or the quality or state of being insubordinate, defiance of authority. It is individual resistance to military authority; any act, language, or disobedience in defiance of authority.

Insurgency

Armed rebellion by a section of population against the legally constituted Government, with the support or sympathy of the local population, obtained voluntarily or by coercion. It covers the full spectrum from subversion to full-scale guerilla war, including the emergence of guerilla bands into regular units. Insurgency is also defined as a civil commotion caused by an armed violence within the territory of a sovereign State.

Intelligibly

That can be easily understood. *See* Army Rule 52(1).

Intended

Designed or contemplated; intentional. *See* Army Rule 30(4).

Intent to Defraud

The term contains two elements, deceit and injury. The first element of deceit could also show an intention to deceive or in some cases mere secrecy.

Intentionally

Done deliberately or something that was intended. The court may infer intention from the circumstances proved in evidence. As a general rule, a person is presumed in law to have intended the natural and probable consequence of his act.

Intentional Misconduct

It does not include a mere error in Judgment. [US MCM IV-35.]

Inter-alia

Among other things.

Internal Defence

The full range of measures taken by a Government to free and protect its society from subversion, lawlessness and insurgency.

Internal Disturbances

Situations in which there is no non-international armed conflict as such, but there consists a confrontation within the country, which is characterised by a certain seriousness or duration and which involves acts of violence. These latter can assume various forms, all the way from the spontaneous generation of acts of revolt to the struggle between more or less organised groups and the authorities in power. In these situations, which do not necessarily degenerate into open struggle, the authorities in power call upon extensive police forces, or even armed forces, to restore internal order. The high number of victims has made necessary the application of a minimum of humanitarians rules.

Internal Security

The role of the defence services, in which they are required to assist the civil authorities, in maintaining law and order within the country. The state of law and order prevailing within a nation.

Internal Security Column

A special body of troops, kept in readiness to move at a short notice, to any threatened point in the town at which the troops forming the column are located.

Internal Tensions

A situation of serious tension (political, religious, racial, social, economic etc.) or sequels of an armed conflict or internal disturbances.

Internally Displaced Persons

Persons or groups of persons who have been forced to flee their homes or places of habitual residence suddenly or unexpectedly as a result of armed conflict, internal strife, systematic violations of human rights or natural or man-made disasters, and who have not crossed an internationally recognised State Border.

International Armed Conflict

Refers to all cases of declared war or of any other armed conflict which may arise between two or more of the High Contracting Parties, even if the state of war is not recognised by one of them, or all cases of partial or total occupation of the territory of a High Contracting Party, even if the said occupation meets with no armed resistance. The term includes military occupation. International armed conflict and war are synonymous terms. They both refer to armed conflicts between States, including situations of armed conflict regarded by only one State Party as international.

International Custom

Article 38.1b of the ICJ Statute defines the term as evidence of a general practice accepted as law.

International Customary Law

State practice accepted as legally binding by the subjects of international law.

International Fact Finding Commission

The establishment of a commission consisting of 15 members of high moral standing and acknowledged impartiality is provided for in AP 1, Article 90.

International Human Rights Law

Is a set of international rules, established by treaty or custom, on the basis of which individuals and groups can expect and/ or claim certain behaviour or benefits from Governments. Numerous non-treaty based principles and guidelines ("soft law") also belong to the body of international human rights standards.

International Humanitarian Law

Those international rules, established by treaty or custom, which are specifically intended to solve humanitarian problems directly arising from international or non-international armed conflicts and which, for humanitarian reasons, limit the right of parties to a conflict to use methods and means of warfare of their choice or protect persons and property that are, or may be, affected by the conflict. It protects persons and property, that are, or may be affected by an armed conflict and limits the rights of the parties to a conflict to use methods and means of warfare of their choice.

International Law

Legal system governing relations between entities endowed with international personality.

International Transfer

The transfer, shipment or other movement, of whatever form, of arms from or across the territory of a Contracting Party. *See* Article 7 of the Draft Framework Convention on International Arms Transfer.

Interned in a Foreign Country

A person is interned if he or she is definitely known to have been taken into custody of a non belligerent foreign power as the result of and for reasons arising out of any armed conflict in which own armed forces are engaged.

Internee

One who is interned or confined, especially in war time.

Internment

Or administrative detention is defined as the deprivation of liberty of a person that has been initiated/ordered by the executive branch – not the judiciary – without criminal charges being brought against the internee/administrative detainee. The definition does not include the lawful pre-trial detention of a person held on criminal charges, whether in or outside armed conflict. The term is also intended to cover the notion of 'assigned residence', to which identical provision of the Fourth Geneva Convention apply. It is a measure of control aimed at dealing with persons who pose a real threat to State security, currently or in future, in situations of armed conflict, or to State security or public order in non-conflict situations; it is not a measure that is meant to replace criminal proceedings.

Interposition force

International force the function of which is to place itself physically between parties to a conflict, and, thus to keep them separated.

Interpret

To explain, to translate into intelligible language. *See* Army Rule 23.

Interpreter

He may be appointed to assist the court when any evidence is given in a language which the court or the accused does not understand. He will be sworn or affirmed as such. *See* Army Rules 107 to 109 and Note 4 to Army Act, section 116.

Interrogation

Includes any formal or informal questioning in which an incriminating response either is sought or is a reasonable consequence of such questioning. [US MRE 305(g)(2)(A).]

Interrogatories

Are particular questions in writing, demanded of witnesses or parties brought in to be examined in a case. *See* Army Act, section 138(1).

Interruption

An adverse obstruction. *See* Army Act, section 59(e).

Intervention

Stepping in, interfering in any affair, so as to affect its course or issue. *See* Army Act, section 79.

Intoxication

This is an offence punishable under section 48 of the Army Act. Intoxication may be induced by opium or any similar drug, as well as by liquor. A person is said to be intoxicated if owing to the influence of alcohol or any drug, whether alone or in combinations with any other circumstances, he is unfit to be entrusted with his duty, or any duty, which he may be called upon to perform or behaves in a disorderly manner, or in any manner likely to bring discredit to the service.

Intra Vires

Within the jurisdiction.

Invalid

The word 'invalid' has precisely the same meaning as the words not valid. It means no force or without legal force. In relation to a sentence, it means a punishment which is authorised under the Army Act but is inapplicable in relation to the accused or of the offence with which he is charged.

Invalid Sentence

The words 'invalid sentence' are used to mean a sentence which is authorised under Army Act but which is inapplicable in relation to the accused or to the offence with which he is charged. It is distinct from an illegal sentence which is unknown to the Army Act, *e.g.*, reproof. *See* Note 3 to Army Act, section 163.

Invalidating Board

The recommendation of invalidating board has to precede the decision of discharge. This board has to be held in terms of Army Rule 13(3)1(ii) for persons below officer rank to assess whether a person is unfit for further service on medical grounds. If a person has been found medically invalid for further service, an order of discharge can be passed only on the recommendation of an invalidating board.

Invalidity

The state of being unable to take care because of illness or injury. The state of not being legally or officially acceptable. *See* Army Rule 103.

Invasion

Invasion is not necessarily occupation, although as a rule occupation will be coincident with invasion. Reconnoitring parties, flank guards, raiding or flying columns and similar bodies which move on or retire after carrying out their special mission cannot, however, be said to occupy the country which they have traversed. They certainly occupy every locality of which they are in possession and where they set up a temporary administration, but such occupation ceases the moment they move on or retire.

Investigation

In the sense of ascertainment of facts, means, sifting of materials and search for relevant data. It connotes a minute inquiry, a scrutiny; a strict examination. *See* Army Act, section 50(a). Investigation connotes a minute inquiry; a scrutiny; a strict examination. It includes all the proceedings under the Cr PC for the collection of evidence conducted by a police officer or by any person other than a Magistrate; who is authorised by a Magistrate in this behalf.

Involuntary

A statement is "involuntary" if it is obtained in violation of the self incrimination privilege or due process, or through the use of coercion, unlawful influence, or unlawful inducement.

Irregular

Units, other than those of the regular Army and embodied Territorial Army, who may be used in any combat role. Not normal, not according to the usual rules. *See* RA(DSR), para 539.

Irregular Corps

Any force (other than the Regular Forces or the Territorial Army or the National Cadet Corps) raised and maintained in India under the authority of the Central Government, or any other force which may be notified in this behalf by order published in the Official Gazette. *See* section 2(1) of the Indian Tolls (Army and Air Force) Act, 1901.

Irregular Order

An order is irregular if the procedure followed is in violation of the principles of natural justice and fair play.

Items

Material equipment, and technology, of any description, notified under this Act or any other Act related to relevant activity.

See section 4(f) of the Weapons of Mass Destruction and their Delivery Systems(Prohibition of Unlawful Activities) Act, 2005.

J

JCO

A class of junior leaders in the Army. Junior Commissioned Officers means a person commissioned, gazetted or in pay as a junior commissioned officer. The JCO ranks in order of precedence are Risaldar Major or Subedar Major, Risaldar or Subedar and Naib Risaldar or Naib Subedar.

Joint Staff

A staff formed of two or more of the services of the country.

Joint Trial

Is the trial by court-martial of more than one accused who are tried together for an offence averred to have been committed by them collectively. *See* Army Rule 35.

Judge Advocate

An individual appointed for every general court-martial for the trial of military personnel accused of a breach of the Articles of War. He is appointed by the convening authority and must be relieved by the same authority. He advises court on points of law, of custom, and of form, and invites their attention to any deviation therefrom. He must be present at the court for which he is appointed, not only to record all its proceedings but also in order to impart validity to its jurisdiction. If any question of law arises out of the proceedings, and he is called upon for his opinion, he is bound to give it.

Judge Advocate-General

Government functionary who acts as the legal adviser of the Government in matters touching military law, the supreme judge in martial law as to the jurisdiction and power of military courts, but neither a judge nor a juror as to the charge. He is registrar of courts-martial.

Judge Martial

Also called Advocate-General, is the supreme judge in martial law as to the jurisdiction and powers of military courts. It is incumbent upon this person as well as upon his deputies to be well acquainted with the laws of the land, that they may admonish the court or the president when their proceedings are tending to infringe the civil law.

Judgments

The cognizance which is taken and the sentence that are passed for military offences. Binding settlement of a dispute by a judicial tribunal. *See* Army Act, section 81(1).

Judicial Notice

The term means that court will recognise a matter without formal evidence. A court can take judicial notice, of any facts which are assumed to be so generally known as not to require special proof. The courts are expressly authorised to take judicial notice of all matters of notoriety, including all matters within their general military knowledge.

Judicial or Other Authority

Means a judicial or other authority under the law whose status and tenure should afford the strongest possible guarantees of competence, impartiality and independence. *See* Scope of the Body of the Principles, adopted by GA Resolution 43/173 of 9 Dec 1988; Code of Conduct for Law Enforcement Officials, Adopted by General Assembly Resolution 34/169 of 17 Dec 1979.

Judicial Proceedings

It includes a proceeding before any court, tribunal or person having, by law, power to hear, receive and examine evidence on oath. For the course authorised to be taken in various cases to secure the determination of controversy, to obtain the enforcement of a right or the redress or prevention of a wrong. *See* Army Act, section 152.

Judicial Settlement

Adjudication of a dispute by a permanent judicial institution.

Jurisdiction

Legal authority, extent of power. The jurisdiction of a military court does not depend on where or against whom an offence took place, but on the status of the accused person, that is whether he is or not a person subject to military law. Jurisdiction means the power to hear a case and to render a legally competent decision.

Jury

Makeshift, temporary, a body of persons sworn to declare the truth on evidence before them.

Jus ad bellum

The rules governing the use of force. It deals with the legality of the decision to engage in the use of armed force.

Jus in bello

Deals with facts, with the fact of an armed clash, irrespective of what caused the conflict and whether it can be said to have any justification. It deals with the means and methods of warfare employed by adversaries once they are engaged in an armed conflict.

Juvenile Offender

The United Nations Standard Minimum Rules for the Administration of Juvenile Justice (Beijing Rules) define a juvenile as a child or young person who, under the respective legal systems, may be dealt with for an offence in a manner which different from an adult [Rule 2.2(a)]. Under the Beijing Rules, a juvenile offender is a child or young person who is alleged to have committed or who has been found to have committed an offence [Rule 2.2(c)].

K

King's Regulations

These were approved by the King by virtue of his Royal prerogative, and issued by the Army Council for general guidance throughout the Army, to be strictly observed on all occasions.

Knowingly

With knowledge, consciously, intelligently, wilfully, intentionally. An individual acts knowingly when he acts with awareness of the nature of his conduct. The term signifies knowledge of the facts material to the offender's guilt.

L

LAC

This is an imaginary line based on geography features drawn between two opposing forces which denote the area actually controlled on the ground by opposing forces by effective fire, observation or by patrols. This line is neither delineated nor demarcated. In our context, it refers to our disputed border with China.

Landing Place

It includes a pier, wharf, quay, jetty and a stage, whether fixed or floating. *See* section 2(h) of the Indian Tolls (Army and Air Force) Act, 1901.

Lapse

Fail, to come to an end, fault or error.

Law Enforcement Officials

The term includes all officers of the law, whether appointed or elected, who exercise police powers, especially the powers of arrest or detention. In countries where police powers are exercised by military authorities, whether uniformed or not, or by State Security forces the definition of law enforcement officials shall be regarded as including officers of such services.

Law of Arms

Certain acknowledged rules, regulations, and precepts, which relate to war, and are observed by all civilized nations. These are precepts showing how to proclaim war, to attack the enemy, and to punish offenders in the camp; also restricting the contending parties from certain cruelties etc.

Law of Arms Control

Is set out in disarmament agreements providing for the reduction or even the elimination of a certain weapon potential. Reciprocity is an important consideration in any disarmament agreement, and humanitarian concerns a secondary factor.

Law of Hague

It regulates methods and means of warfare – prohibitions against using certain weapons such as poison humanitarian concerns such as warning the civilian population before a bombardment and the law of belligerent occupation, particularly with respect to property.

Law of War

That part of international law which regulates the conduct of armed hostilities. It is often called the law of armed conflict. The law of war encompasses all international law for the conduct of hostilities binding on a State or its individual citizens, including treaties and international agreements and applicable customary international law.

Lawful Command

The term relates to a command which is specific to an individual and justified by military, as well as by civil law and usage. In other words, a lawful military command, whether to do or not to do, or to desist from doing, a particular act. It must relate to military duty and must have reference to the time at which the command is to be obeyed. *See* Note 3 to Army Act, section 41. The disobedience of it must tend to impede, delay or prevent a military proceeding.

Legal Cell

These are offices set up at the location of the Supreme Court or the High Courts or at any other location to assist in disposal of pending cases involving application of law.

Legal Officer

Any commissioned officer of the Navy, Marine Corps, or Coast Guard designated to perform legal duties of a command under UCMJ.

Legality

The fact of being legal, lawfulness. *See* Army Act, section 164(1).

Legation

A diplomatic mission in a foreign country headed by a minister. *See* RA(DSR), para 558.

Legitimacy

The fact of being legitimate.

Legitimate

Lawful, for which there is a fair and acceptable reason. *See* RA(DSR), para 836(b).

Letters Rogatory

A customary method of obtaining evidence abroad, it takes the form of a letter request from a judicial official of one nation to a court, officer or agency of another nation seeking assistance in the performance of an investigative act. The decision to render assistance, however, is purely discretionary.

Levee en Masse

This occurs when inhabitants of a non-occupied territory, who on the approach of the enemy spontaneously take up arms to resist the invading forces, without having had time to form themselves into regular armed units, provided they carry arms openly and respect the laws and customs of war. *See* GC II, Article 4(A).

Levy, To

Has three distinct military acceptations, as to levy or raise an army; to levy or make war; and to levy contributions.

Liabilities

Amounts of money owned to others for goods and services received, or for assets acquired. Liabilities include accrued amounts earned but not yet due for payment, and progress payments due to contractors. *See* RA(DSR), paras 809(c) and 838.

Lieber Code

It provides a documentary foundation for further development of the law of war and identifies military necessity as a general legal principle to limit violence. It has often been called the earliest official Government codification of the laws of war.

Lien

A charge on property for the payment of a debt or duty. *See* RA(DSR), para 809.

Limit

Restriction, the greatest or smallest amount of some thing that is allowed, a point at which something stops being possible or existing. *See* Army Act, section 81.

Limited War

Any conflict between two or more nations that is short of total war, and is conducted within limitations accepted by or imposed on both sides.

Lingerer

One who pretends to be indisposed, in order to avoid his tour of duty.

Link Sign

A group of letters or letters and figures that identifies a radio link and is used in calling and answering.

Liquidated Damages

Damages the amount of which is ascertained.

Literal Interpretation

Interpretation of words in accordance with their usual or strict meaning.

Litispendence

Period during which a law suit is going on before a court.

Local Order

These are orders issued and applicable to a distinct geographical area or a unit. Their disobedience may constitute an offence under section 42(e) of the Army Act.

Local Rank

Local ranks, appropriate to the appointments held, may be granted to officers, if considered necessary, in the interest of service. *See* RA(DSR), para 88.

Local rank or temporary rank, also means an officer who receives increased rank, for a limited period or during the performance of some specific duty. Also sometimes applied to an officer who is assigned to duty by his brevet rank to a locality fixed by geographical limits, such as a military department or district.

Local Stores

Are articles of indigenous produce or manufacture as distinct from imported stores.

Logical Interpretation

Interpretation of a document in accordance with formal and, apparently logical, criteria of reasoning.

Loiter

To stand around, to move about slowly, to linger, or to lag behind when that conduct is in violation of known instructions or accompanied by a failure to give complete attention to duty.

Looting or Pillaging

Unlawfully seizing or appropriating property which is located in enemy or occupied territory.

Loss

Or damage, means a total or partial elimination of equipment and/or supplies resulting from:

(a) A no fault incident.
(b) The actions of one or more belligerents.
(c) A decision approved by the Force Commander.

Loss Certificate

A document prepared to get any loss of funds or property regularized by seeking orders of the competent financial authority.

Loss of Proceedings

Military law contains suitable provisions to be adopted in the event of loss of original proceedings which require confirmation. [Army Rule 148.]

Low Intensity Conflict

LIC encompasses a variety of violent and low-level conflict situations. In most cases, such conflicts fall under the category of politico-military confrontation between contending states or groups. Such conflicts are at a much lower scale than conventional war but are above the routine and peaceful competitions among states. One of the parties to the conflict may not be State, as in an insurgency situation. It frequently involves protracted struggle of competing principles and ideologies. LIC ranges from high grade internal struggle situations to the extensive employment of the Armed Forces in counter insurgency operations. It is waged by a combination of means, employing political, economic, informational and military instruments. It includes terrorism but excludes purely criminal acts.

Lunatic

Person of unsound mind, affected with lunacy. He is one who had understanding, but, by disease, grief, or other accident, has lost the use of reason. *See* Army Act, sections 148 and 149.

M

Maintenance

(a) Maintenance includes all action taken for retaining an item in or restoring it to a serviceable condition. It includes inspection, testing, servicing, modification, overhaul, conditioning and classification as to serviceability, repair, rebuilding and reclamation. Maintenance can be classified as preventive maintenance and corrective maintenance.

(b) All supply and repair action taken to keep a force in condition to carry out its mission.

(c) The routine recurring work required to keep a facility (plant, building, structure, ground facility, utility system, or other real property) in such condition that it may be continuously utilised, at its original or designed capacity and efficiency, for its intended purpose.

Major Disaster

Natural catastrophe (including any hurricane, tornado, storm, high water, wind driven water, tidal wave, tsunami, earthquake, volcanic eruption, landslide, mudslide, snowstorm, or drought), or regardless of cause, any fire, flood or explosion, in any part, which causes damage of sufficient severity and magnitude to warrant major disaster assistance.

'Make' Decision

Capital acquisitions covered under the decision for indigenous production and research and development.

Malicious

A communication is malicious if the accused believed that the information would probably interfere with the peaceful use of the building, vehicle, aircraft, or other property concerned, or would cause fear or concern to one or more persons.

Malicious Injury to Property

The essence of the offence is injury to the property of another. It is immaterial whether the offender is himself benefitted by the act or not. Such acts are offences if done unlawfully and maliciously. A person is considered to cause an injury unlawfully and maliciously if he wilfully causes it without any lawful excuse *i.e.*, if he causes it by an act which he must know will probably cause it, or is reckless whether he causes it or not, and if he has not either a legal right to act as he does, or a bonafide and reasonable belief that he has such a right. Generally speaking, the act itself justifies a presumption of malice until the contrary is shown, *e.g.*, that it was due to negligence or accident.

Malinger

To malinger is to pretend illness or infirmity which does not exist, in order to escape duty. *See* Note 8 to Army Act, section 46.

Maltreat

To be very cruel to a person or animal. *See* Army Act, section 64(a).

Maltreatment

It must be real, although not necessarily physical, and it must be without justifiable cause. Abuse of an inferior by inflammatory and derogatory words may, through mental anguish, constitute this offence. *See* US MCM IV-43.

Management

The act of running and controlling a business or similar organization. *See* Army Act, section 177(a).

Mandate

An official order given to somebody to perform a particular task.

Manifest Injury

It does not mean minor inconvenience or expense.

Manslaughter

It is the unjustifiable and inexcusable killing of a human being by a person having the necessary criminal capacity, but without malice either express or implied. It is unlawful homicide without malice afterthought.

Manual

Book of reference.

Manual of Court-Martial

One of the main sources of military law jurisprudence in the United States, MCM was promulgated by executive order of the President, has been revised frequently, most recently in 2002. It includes specifications for Uniform Code of Military Justice (UCMJ) crimes, Rules for Courts Martial (RCM), Military Rules of Evidence (MRE), and analysis of the code and rules.

Maritime Frontier

Limit of the territorial sea.

Marking of Exhibits

As pages of court-martial proceedings are marked "A" to "J", the convening order will be marked "K". Other exhibits produced should be marked in the top right hand corner with the letters "L" to "Z", then "AA" to "ZZ" in the order in which produced. *See* Para 7 of the Notes on Military and Air Force Law.

Martial Law

Suspension of civil administration and Government by military administration. It means the suspension of ordinary law and Government of a country (or part of it) by military tribunals of its own Army.

Mass Punishments

In the training academies, following mass punishments may be resorted to under special situations at the discretion of the Commandant—

(a) Route marches

(b) Map Reading/adventure/tactical exercises

(c) Running to be confined to the training areas/parade grounds/company/battalion lines.

Material of Civil Defence Organisation

Equipments, supplies and transports used by these organisations for the performance of the tasks mentioned.

[Article 61(4) – Protocol Additional to the Geneva Conventions of 12 August, 1949, and relating to the Protection of Victims of International Armed Conflicts (Protocol I), 8 June, 1977.]

Matter in Aggravation

Any circumstance serving to explain the commission of the offence, including the reasons that motivated the accused, but not extending to a legal justification.

Matter in Mitigation

Any circumstance which is introduced for the purpose of lessening the punishment to be awarded by a court or to serve as grounds for a reduction of that sentence in clemency.

Medal

A decoration awarded to a soldier for outstanding bravery or for exceptional achievement; a piece of metal in the form of a coin.

Medical Aircraft

Any medical transports by air.

[Article 8(j) – Protocol Additional to the Geneva Conventions of 12 August, 1949, and Relating to the Protection of Victims of International Armed Conflicts (Protocol I), 8 June, 1977.]

Medical Personnel

Those persons assigned, by a Party to the conflict, exclusively to the medical purposes enumerated under (e) or to the administration of medical units or to the operation or administration of medical transports. Such assignments may be either permanent or temporary. The term includes:

(i) medical personnel of a Party to the conflict, whether military or civilian, including those described in the First and Second Conventions, and those assigned to civil defence organisations;

(ii) medical personnel of national Red Cross (Red Crescent, Red Lion and Sun) Societies and other national voluntary aid societies duly recognised and authorised by a Party to the conflict;

(iii) medical personnel or medical units or medical transports described in Article 9, paragraph 2.

[Article 8(c) – Protocol Additional to the Geneva Conventions of 12 August, 1949, and Relating to the Protection of Victims of International Armed Conflicts (Protocol I), 8 June, 1977.]

Medical Ships and Craft

Any medical transports by water.

[Article 8(i) – Protocol Additional to the Geneva Conventions of 12 August, 1949, and Relating to the Protection of Victims of International Armed Conflicts (Protocol I), 8 June, 1977.]

Medical Transports

Any means of transportation, whether military or civilian, permanent or temporary, assigned exclusively to medical transportation and under the control of a competent authority of a Party to the conflict.

[Article 8(g) – Protocol Additional to the Geneva Conventions of 12 August, 1949, and Relating to the Protection of Victims of International Armed Conflicts (Protocol I), 8 June, 1977.]

Medical Transportation

The conveyance by land, water or air of the wounded, sick, shipwrecked, medical personnel, religious personnel, medical equipment or medical supplies protected by the conventions and by the undermentioned Protocol.

[Article 8(f) – Protocol Additional to the Geneva Conventions of 12 August, 1949, and Relating to the Protection of Victims of International Armed Conflicts (Protocol I), 8 June, 1977.]

Medical Units

Establishments and other units, whether military or civilian, organised for medical purposes, namely the search for, collection, transportation, diagnosis or treatment – including first-aid treatment – of the wounded, sick and shipwrecked, or for the prevention of disease. The term includes for example, hospitals and other similar units, blood transfusion centres, preventive medicine centres and institutes, medical depots and the medical and pharmaceutical stores of such units. Medical units may be fixed or mobile, permanent or temporary. *See* Article 8(e) AP I.

Medical Vehicles

Any medical transports by land.

[Article 8(h) –Protocol Additional to the Geneva Conventions of 12 August, 1949, and relating to the Protection of Victims of International Armed Conflicts (Protocol I), 8 June, 1977.]

Members

Officers are so called who are detailed by orders to sit on courts-martial.

Memorandum

A record of a legal agreement which has not yet been formally prepared and signed or a proposal or report on a particular subject for a person, organisation, a committee etc. A brief note in writing of some transaction. *See* Army Rule 130.

Memorandum of Agreement or Memorandum of Understanding

A written agreement between Governments or a Government and international organisation signed by authorised representatives and signifying an intent to be legally bound.

Menaces

Include threats of injury to persons or property, and threats which would involve injury to a third person intended to be injured, such as would induce a person to whom the menaces are addressed to part with money or valuable property.

Mental Disorder

A disease of the mind. *See* section 2 of the Canada's National Defence Act, 1985.

Mercenary

Soldiers serving for pay in a foreign service. Mercenaries are not regular members of the Armed Forces, they are paid at higher rates than such members, and take part in hostilities only for "private gain". They enroll voluntarily out of love of money and a spirit of adventure. They cannot claim prisoner of war status. A mercenary is any person who:

(a) is specially recruited locally or abroad in order to fight in an armed conflict;

(b) does, in fact, take a direct part in the hostilities;

(c) is motivated to take part in the hostilities essentially by the desire for private gain and, in fact, is promised, by or on behalf of a Party to the conflict, material compensation substantially in excess of that promised or paid to combatants of similar ranks and functions in the armed forces of that Party;

(d) is neither a national of a Party to the conflict nor a resident of territory controlled by a Party to the conflict;

(e) is not a member of the armed forces of a Party to the conflict; and

(f) has not been sent by a State which is not a Party to the conflict on official duty as a member of its armed forces.

[Article 47(2), Protocol Additional to the Geneva Conventions of 12 August, 1949, and Relating to the Protection of Victims of International Armed Conflicts (Protocol I), 8 June, 1977.]

Mercy

A kind or forgiving attitude towards somebody that you have the power to harm or right to punish. *See* Army Rule 66.

Merits

In practice a matter of substance, as distinguished from matter of form, the real or substantial grounds of action or defence, in contra-distinction to some technical or collateral matter. Decision upon merit means a decision not merely upon formal points.

Military

Pertaining to any one or more of the Armed Services whether Army, Navy or Air Force.

Military Advantage

May relate to the overall military operation and not merely to a single sortie or attack.

See HPCR Draft Manual on Air and Missile Warfare.

Military Convict

Person under sentence of penal servitude passed by a court-martial.

Military Custody

Arrest or confinement of a person according to the usages of the service and includes naval or air force custody. *See* Army Act, section 3(xiii).

Military Discipline

It is the duty of all ranks to uphold the good reputation of service. Any act, conduct or neglect, therefore, which amounts to a failure in that duty by an individual may well prejudice military discipline, although it has no direct bearing on the discipline of the unit to which the offender belongs. *See* Notes to Army Act, section 63.

Military Duty

Every duty which an officer or enlisted person may legally be required by superior authority to execute is necessarily a military duty. [US MCM IV-35(c)(2).]

Military Effort

Any military activities undertaken for the conduct of hostilities.

Military Execution

The punishment inflicted by the sentence of a court-martial.

Military Forces

The whole body of soldiers, soldiery, militia, the Army, connected with the soldiers or armed forces.

Military Government Court

A military court set up by a military Government in occupied territory to exercise jurisdiction over all persons, except members of occupying and allied forces who are subject to military law in respect of matters assigned to them by the proclamation ordinances, laws and orders promulgated by the commander-in-chief or by a military Government for military purposes or for the maintenance of public order and safety.

Military Judge

The commissioned officer who acts as the judge in courts-martial. Under Canada's National Defence Act, 1985, the Governor-in-Council may appoint officers who are barristers or advocates of at least ten years standing at the bar of a province to be military judges. A military judge holds office during good behaviour for a term of five years but may be removed by the Governor-in-Council for cause on the recommendation of an Inquiry Committee established under regulations by the Governor-in-Council. A military judge is eligible to be reappointed on the expiry of a first or subsequent term of office on the recommendation of a Renewal Committee established under regulations made by the Governor-in-Council. A Military judge ceases to hold office on reaching the retirement age prescribed by Governor-in-Council in regulations. Military Judges shall preside at courts-martial and shall perform other judicial duties under the above Act that are required to be performed by them. In addition, they shall perform any other duties that the Chief Military Judge may direct, but those other duties may not be incompatible with their judicial duties. They may, with the concurrence of Chief Military Judge, be appointed as a board of inquiry.

Military Law

A branch of the general municipal law, consisting of the rules ordained for the Government of the military forces of a state or Government, and those voluntarily serving with them, equally in peace and war, and administered by tribunals of special and limited jurisdiction. It is the law which governs officers and soldiers in peace and war, at home and abroad.

Military Necessity

It is one of the principles governing use of force. There must be justification for each separate act. Action should not be taken in one place with the object of creating effect in another place. There should be no reprisal. Action should be preventive and not punitive. Military necessity is defined as those measures which are indispensable for securing the ends of war, and which are lawful according to the modern law and usages of war.

Military Objectives

So far as objects are concerned, any object which by its nature, location, purpose or use makes an effective contribution to military action and whose total or partial destruction, capture or neutralization, in the circumstances ruling at the time, offers a definite military advantage.

[Article 52(2) AP I.]

Military Offence

Are those offences which are strictly military in nature or those which are denounced by military law rather severely because of the nature of military duty and martial responsibilities.

Military Officers

A person, who being an officer within the meaning of the Army Act, 1950, the Navy Act, 1957, or the Air Force Act, 1950, is commissioned, gazetted or in pay as an officer doing army, naval or air force duty with the Army, Navy or Air Force, or is an officer doing such duty in any arm, branch or part of any of these forces. *See* section 2(xxi) of the Cantonment Act, 1924.

Military Operations

Refers to all movements and acts related to hostilities that are undertaken by armed forces. These are a series of warlike or strategic acts and battles and manoeuvres of all kinds, taken as a whole, as carried out by armed forces in a defined area. Activity aimed at achieving a specific objective related to the conduct of hostilities or, in other words, a specific military advantage.

Military Operations Other Than War

Operations that encompass the use of military capabilities across the military operations short of war. These military actions can be applied to compliment any combination of the other instruments of national power and occur before, during and after war. *See* USA DoD Directory of Military and Associated Terms – Joint Chiefs of Staff Publication.

Military Prison

A building or part of a building set apart as such under the military law provisions.

Military Prisoner

A person under sentence of imprisonment passed by a court-martial.

Military Property

It is all property, real or personal, owned, held or used by one of the armed forces.

Military Receivable Order

These are used for paying money into a Government treasury or bank which shall show distinctly the nature of the payment, the person or officer on whose account it is made and the particular controller of Defence Accounts by whom it is adjustable.

Military Reward

Includes any gratuity or annuity for long service or good conduct, good service pay, pension, and any other military pecuniary award. *See* Army Act, section 3(xiv). A war gratuity is thus a military reward.

Military Station

A place calculated for the rendezvous of troops, or for distribution of them.

Militia

The domestic force for the defence of a nation, as distinguished from the regular Army, which can be employed at home or abroad in either aggressive or defensive operations.

Mine

Any munition placed under, on or near the ground or other surface area and designed to be detonated or exploded by the presence, proximity or contact of a person or vehicle, and "remotely delivered mine" means any mine so defined delivered by artillery, rocket, mortar or similar means or dropped from an aircraft.

[Article 2(1), Protocol on Prohibitions or Restrictions on the Use of Mines, Booby-Traps and Other Devices (Protocol II), Geneva, 10 October, 1980.]

Mined Area

Is an area which is dangerous due to the presence of the mines. *See* Article 2 of Protocol on Prohibitions or Restrictions on the Use of Mines, Booby-Traps and Other Devices as Amended on 3 May, 1996.

Minefield

Is a defined area in which mines have been emplaced. The term minefield includes phoney minefields. *See* Article 2 of Protocol on Prohibitions or Restrictions on the Use of Mines, Booby-Traps and Other Devices as Amended on 3 May, 1996.

Minimum Force

It is one of the principles governing use of force. No more force is to be used than is necessary to achieve the immediate effect. This refers to the actual amount of force used and not to the number of troops employed.

Minor Offence

Under UCMJ, it is an offence for which confinement of less than one year is authorised.

Minorities

Ethnic, linguistic, national or religious groups which are different from the majority of the population of a country.

Misbehaves

The term in the context of Army Act, section 34(c), means that the accused from an un-soldier like regard for his personal safety, failed in respect of some distinct and feasible duty imposed upon him by specified order or regulation, or by the well understood custom of the service or by the requirements of the case, as applicable to the position in which he was placed at the time.

Miscarriage of Justice

Prejudicial to substantial rights of a party, a situation in which a court makes a wrong decision, especially when somebody is punished when they are innocent. *See* Army Rule 35(4).

Misconduct

Wrong or improper conduct, *i.e.*, conduct in violation of a definite rule of action. It means malfeasance, improper conduct. It cannot be read as synonymous with negligence but involves a greater degree of culpability. It is the intentional doing of something which the doer knows to be wrong or which he does recklessly not caring what the result may be. *See* Army Act, section 91(d). The word receives its connotation from the context of delinquency in its performance and its effect on the discipline and the nature of the duty. It may involve moral turpitude, it must be improper or wrong behaviour, wilful in character; forbidden act, a transgression of established and definite rule of action or code of conduct but not mere error of judgment, carelessness or negligence in performance of the duty; the act complained of bears forbidden quality of character. See *UOI* v. *Harjeet Singh Sandhu*, Mil LJ 2001 SC 10.

Misdemeanor

A crime punishable by fine and rigorous or simple imprisonment at the discretion of court.

Misuse

Improper, unlawful or incorrect use. Mis-application.

Missing

Is defined as a person who is not present at his or her duty location due to apparent involuntary reasons and whose location is unknown.

Missing in Action

Is defined as the involuntary absence of a person whose location is unknown, and

(a) the absence is a result of a hostile action; or

(b) the absence is under circumstances suggesting it is a result of hostile action.

Mitigate

Awarding a less amount of the same species of punishment, as for example, by reducing the length of imprisonment to which an offender has been sentenced and is in effect equivalent tot a remission of the part of the sentence. The power to mitigate etc. cannot be exercised whilst execution of the sentence is suspended.

Mixed Courts

Such as Special Court for Sierra Leone, established in recent years, comprise elements of both international and domestic jurisdiction.

Mixed Pleas

Where an accused pleads guilty to some charges in the charge-sheet and not guilty to others.

Mobilization

Transition of the armed forces from peace time to war time tables of organisation and equipment. Mobilization deployment includes, bringing units up to strength with personnel, combat material, armament and transport, providing troops with all types of personal belongings, rations and provisions, fuels and lubricants etc. It is the process by which the armed forces or a part thereof are expanded and brought to a state of readiness for war or other national emergency.

Moderation

The quality of being reasonable and not being extreme. *See* Army Rule 77(2).

Modified Field Area

Is an area where troops are deployed in support of combat echelons, troops in an operational support role. Degree of operational readiness is slightly lower than that of field area, though sustained surveillance continues. Such areas would also cover geographically isolated areas, with long and tenuous lines of communications and areas with inadequate infrastructural facilities.

Money

The term includes coin, bank notes or currency notes. Money orders and postal orders are not "money" but "valuable securities".

Moral Turpitude

Must be imputed with the act constituting offence which is dishonest or immoral, or conduct which is so unethical as to render the offender unfit to hold the office. See *Thakorbhai Bhagabhai* v. *DDO, Surat,* 1980 (3) SLR Guj 535 (Para 7).

Motion

A motion for appropriate relief is a request for ruling to cure a defect which deprives a party of a right or hinders a party from preparing for trial or presenting its case. [US RCM 906(a).]

Motion to Dismiss

It is a request to terminate further proceedings as to one or more charges and specifications on grounds capable of resolution without trial of the general issue of guilt. [US RCM 907(a).]

Movement

It includes a move, transfer or shift of a ship, aircraft or unit involving a substantial distance and period of time.

Movement Order

An order issued by a commander covering the details for move of one or more of his command.

Multiplicity

A defect in charge whereby a single transaction is made the subject of more than one charge. *See* Note 6 to Army Rule 30.

Municipal Law

Law operating within the State, as distinct from international law.

Munitions of War

Includes the whole or any part of any ship, submarine, aircraft, tank or similar engine, arms and ammunition, torpedo or mine intended or adapted for use in war, and any other article, material, or device, whether actual or proposed, intended for such use. *See* section 2(5) of the Official Secrets Act, 1923.

Murder

Is unlawful homicide with malice afterthought.

Mutilate

To damage severely, especially by violently removing a part, injure, damage or disfigure somebody by breaking, tearing or cutting off a necessary part.

Mutiny

It is one of the offences punishable under section 37 of the Army Act. Mutiny implies collective insubordination, or a combination of two or more persons to resist or to induce others to resist, lawful military authority.

N

Narrative

An account or narration. *See* Army Rule 92(2).

National Command

A command that is organised by, and functions under the authority of a specific nation.

Nationality

Membership of a nation. It is the condition or status of belonging to a Nation or State; either by birth or naturalization.

Nationality Principle

This principle of criminal jurisdiction determines jurisdiction with reference to the nationality or national character of the person committing the offence. In the context of fight against international terrorism it implies that every nation has the authority to establish and enforce criminal laws regarding the conduct of its nationals wherever they are located. Similarly, vessels have the nationality of the nation in which they are registered, and so are subject to that nation's laws. Business corporations have the nationality of the nation in which they were incorporated.

Natural Law

Rules derived from God, reason or nature, as distinct from man-made law.

Naturalisation

The act of adopting a foreigner, and clothing him with the privileges of a native citizen.

Nature of Arrest

The term refers to the type of arrest which may be either open or close.

Naval Establishment

An establishment belonging to, or under the control of, the Indian Navy whether within or without India. *See* Navy Act, section 3(12A).

Naval Tribunal

A court-martial constituted under section 97 and includes a disciplinary court constituted under section 96, a commanding officer or other officer or authority exercising powers of punishment under the Navy Act. *See* section 3(15) of the Navy Act.

NCO

An officer, without a commission, but who by his position in a regiment, and by virtue of the power attached to that position exercises control over the private soldiers. Non-Commissioned Officers are the subordinate officers of the general staff, regiments, and companies who are appointed not by commission, but by the Secretary of War or Commanding Officers of regiments, and they are usually selected on account of good conduct or superior abilities.

Necessities

Habit and desire create necessities. Things that are necessary. Basic necessities, such as food and clothing. *See* Army Rule 36.

Necessity

Necessity is one of the principles that must govern the actions of the command of troops in internal security duties. It implies the following:-

(a) There must be justification for each separate act.

(b) Action should not be taken in one place with the object of creating effect in another place.

(c) There should be no reprisals.

(d) Action should be preventive and not punitive.

Necessity of War

Wartime sovereignty.

Negative Conflict of Jurisdiction

Two or more organs decline jurisdiction although potentially competent.

Neglect

It is the absence of conduct which would have been taken by a reasonably careful person in the same or similar circumstances. [US MCM IV-35.]

Negligence

The failure to exercise the care, prudence, or attention to duties that the interests of the Government require to be exercised by a prudent and reasonable person under the circumstances. The omission to do something which a reasonable man guided upon those considerations which ordinarily regulate the conduct of human affairs would do, or doing something which a prudent and reasonable man would not do so.

Negligently

An act or omission of a person who is under a duty to use due care which exhibits a lack of that degree of care which a reasonably prudent person would have exercised under the same or similar circumstances.

Neutral

A State not party to an international armed conflict.

See HPCR Draft Manual on Air and Missile Warfare.

Neutrality

It necessarily implies impartiality. Not taking sides on the political grounds of a conflict. Status of a Power not at war in relation to the belligerents involving any duty of impartiality on the part of the neutral State. It is a status involving special rights and obligations subject to international law.

Night

The interval between nine at night and six in the morning.

NOK

Closest living relative or relatives who take the personal estate of one who dies intestate; Who by the statute of distributions succeed to the share in the intestate's personal property. *See* Army Rule 15A.

No Fault Incident

An incident resulting from an accidental occurrence or negligent conduct, but not including acts attributable to wilful misconduct or gross negligence, on the part of an operator/ custodian of equipment.

No Man's Land

That area of ground between two opposing forces which are not physically occupied by either, but which both will endeavour to dominate by means of patrols, ambushes, observation and similar methods.

Non Combatants

These can include both civilians and certain military personnel, such as chaplains and medical personnel.

Non Consensual Sexual Offence

Is a sexual offence in which consent by the victim is an affirmative defence or in which the lack of consent is an element of the offence. This term includes rape, forcible sodomy, assault with intent to commit rape or forcible sodomy, indecent assault, and attempts to commit such offences. [US MRE 412(d).]

Non-Confirmation

It is one of the powers exercisable by a confirming authority in relation to the proceedings of a general or district court-martial. The same is entered in and form part of the proceedings. [Army Rule 70.] The result is that there is no conviction or acquittal for the purpose of any subsequent trial. Note 3 to Army Act, section 153.

Non Defended Locality

Following elements are its constituent:—

- The inhabited place must be open for occupation. (This pre-supposes that the inhabited place must be near or in a zone where adverse armed forces are present.)
- All combatants, as well as mobile weapons and mobile military equipment, must have been evacuated.
- No hostile use shall be made of fixed military installations or establishments.
- No acts of hostility shall be committed by the authorities or by the population.
- No activities in support of military operation shall be undertaken.

Article 59, AP I.

Non Effective

The officers or men employed on other duties than regimental, such as in staff appointments and the like. Sick and disabled man also come under this category and so do all officers on half pay, pensioners and superannuated officers. The term is used as primitive or negative of effective.

Non International Armed Conflict

Any situation where, within a State's territory, clear unmistakable hostilities break out between the armed forces and dissident armed forces or other organised armed groups.

Any situation dissident forces or other organised armed groups are under the leadership of a responsible command exercise such control over a part of the territory as to enable them to conduct sustained and concerted military operations and to implement the Protocol (Protocol II). Within the meaning of Additional Protocol II, is one in which both sides have organised armed forces under responsible command that exercises control over a part of the territory of the State, and in which it is possible to implement common Article 3 and the said Protocol.

Non Judicial Punishment

A punishment (such as reprimand, reduction to the next lower grade etc.) imposed by the commanding officer to officers and men of his command for minor offences and infractions of discipline. Disciplinary punishments may be imposed for minor offences without the intervention of a court-martial under Article 15 of UCMJ.

Non Physical Torture

The infliction of mental suffering by creating a sense of anguish and stress by means other than bodily assault.

Non Punitive Disciplinary Measures

These are meant to address minor violations of the military code or other deficiencies. These are viewed as appropriate vehicles for maintaining good order and discipline in the majority of the situations. These are appropriate for such deficiencies as neglect, laziness, inattention and difficulty in adjusting to military life. These are for correction, not for punishment. These could take the form of admonitions (oral or written warnings), counseling, corrective training, withholding of privileges etc.

Non-recordable

The term relates to the entries of the censures awarded by way of administrative action taken and where record is not to be made in the dossier of person concerned.

Non-State Actor

Is a person or entity not acting under the lawful authority of any country.

See section 4(g) of the Weapons of Mass Destruction and their Delivery Systems (Prohibition of Unlawful Activities) Act, 2005.

Non Standard Item

An item of supply determined by standardisation action as not authorised for procurement.

Norm

Rule of conduct.

Notice

Intimation or warning, making something known. *See* Army Rule 50.

Notification

Formal announcement to another party of a legally relevant fact. Means a notification published in the Official Gazette.

Notion of Occupation

Territory is considered occupied when it is actually placed under the authority of the hostile army. The occupation extends only to the territory where such authority has been established and can be exercised. *See* Article 42 of the Hague Regulations.

Nuclear Weapon or other Nuclear Explosive Device

Any nuclear weapon or other nuclear explosive device as may be determined by the Central Government, whose determination in the matter shall be final.

See section 4(h) of the Weapons of Mass Destruction and their Delivery Systems (Prohibition of Unlawful Activities) Act, 2005.

Null

Of no legal force or effect; void, of no binding force or validity. *See* Army Rule 83(2).

O

Oath

The expressions "oath" and "swear", and other expressions relating thereto, include affirmation or declaration, affirm or declare, and expressions relating thereto, in cases where an affirmation or declaration is, by law, allowed instead of an oath.

Obedience

Blind, complete, unquestioning submission to authority. *See* Army Act, section 30.

Obiter Dictum

Any opinion expressed in a Judgment which is not essential for the decision in the case before the court.

Objection

The action of stating something in opposition to a person or thing, an adverse reason, argument or contention. *See* Army Rule 92(3).

Objection to Charge

Before pleading to any charge the accused may object to it on the ground that it does not disclose an offence under the Army Act or as not being in accordance with the Army Rules.

Obligation

The act of binding oneself by a social, legal or moral tie. A duty to make a future payment of money. The duty is incurred as soon as an order is placed, or a contract is awarded for the delivery of the goods and the performance of services. An obligation legally encumbers a specified sum of money which will require an outlay or expenditure in the future.

Obligation to Serve

Under the Canada's National Defence Act, 1985, the enrolment of a person binds the person to serve in the Canadian Forces until the person is, in accordance with regulations, lawfully released.

Obtaining by False Pretences

When a person obtains not only the possession of, but also the property in, goods by fraud, the offence is not theft but obtaining goods by false pretences.

Occupation

Territory is considered occupied when actually placed under the authority of the hostile army. The occupation extends only to the territories where such authority has been established and is in a position to assert itself. [Hague Rules 42.]

Offence

An offence is an act or omission punishable under Army Act and includes a civil offence. *See* Army Act, section 3(xvii).

Offence Report

A document which contains all the details of a summary trial under Army Act, section 80.

Offender

One who commits an offence. A term constantly employed to indicate persons implicated in the commission of crime.

Offer of Violence

Is any defiant act or gesture, which would, if completed, result in violence, *e.g.*, throwing anything at the superior or pointing a loaded firearm at him.

Officer

A person employed to perform any public duty. An officer in a regiment or department who exercises control or command, and executes authority under a commission from the sovereign. Officers in the military are of several denominations and ranks.

Officer Commanding the Area

The officer Commanding any one of the Areas into which India is, for military purposes for the time being, divided or any sub-area which does not form part of any such area which the Central Government may, by notification in the Official Gazette, declare to be area for all or any of the purposes of the Cantonment Act, 1924.

Officer Commanding the Station

Military officer for the time being in command of the forces in a cantonment, or if that officer is the officer commanding the Area or Officer Commanding-in-Chief the Command, the military officer who would be in command of those forces in the absence of the officer commanding the Area and Officer Commanding-in-Chief the command. *See* section 2(xxiv) of the Cantonment Act, 1924.

Officer Under Instruction

The convening officer may detail one or more officer to attend the trial for the purposes of instruction. Such a officer is required to take oath/affirmation as indicated in Army Rule 46.

Omission

The neglect of a legal duty to act.

On-base Civilian Activity

Civilians are subject to restrictions to protect the order, discipline and military readiness of the installation.

On-base Distribution

The sale, distribution and display of publications on a military installation.

On Duty

An individual is considered for the purpose of Travel Regulations to be "On duty" when performing a journey specified by regulations in the interest of public service and not at the request or for the personal convenience or in consequence of the misconduct of the individual concerned. *See* Travel Regulations, Rule 2.

One Man Inquiry

A non formal investigation carried out in a matter only by one officer detailed for the purpose.

Onus

The responsibility for something, a burden, load.

Open Arrest

Arrest is either open or close. An officer in open arrest may take exercise at stated periods within certain limits, which are usually the precincts of the regimental lines or camp; he must not, however, appear out of uniform or at any place of amusement or public resort, nor must he wear sash, sword, belt or spurs.

Opening Address

An address made by the prosecutor explaining the charge and outlining the facts and the evidence which he proposes to call to prove those facts.

Operation

A series of tactical actions (battles, engagements, strikes etc) sequenced and synchronized in time and peace and aimed to accomplish/achieve a desired objective.

Operative Part of Judgment

The part of a Judgment giving the court's decision.

Oppress

To treat somebody in a cruel and unfair way, especially by not giving them the same freedom, rights, etc. as other people. *See* Army Act, section 64(a).

Order

This term, considered in its relation to the army means injunctions emanating from the authority, measures which regulate service. A communication written, oral or by signal, which conveys instructions from a superior to a subordinate.

Order Book

Every company or sub-unit in the service has such a book, in which orders are written for the information of officers and men. Order books are also kept at all military headquarters.

Order of Battle

The arrangement or disposition of the different component parts of an army in one or more lines for the purpose of engaging an enemy.

Orders

Are the instructions, injunctions or commands issued by superior officers.

Orders in Council

Were made by the King in Council under the authority of various Acts of Parliament in the UK.

Orderly Room

The court of the commanding officer, when charges brought against the men of his regiment are investigated, and sentence passed. It is also the office of the commanding officer, from which all orders emanate.

Ordinarily

In a normal way. *See* Army Rule 38.

Ordinary Pay

Rate of pay with increments, if any, but exclusive of deferred pay, to which a soldier is entitled by reason of his rank, appointment, trade group or trade classification. Additional remuneration, such as subsistence, command, special, or field allowance, though covered by the term "pay" does not fall within the meaning of ordinary pay.

Organised Armed Groups

The expression does not mean any armed band acting under a leader. Such armed groups must be structured and possess weapons, and must therefore have a system for allocating authority and responsibility, they must also be subject to rules of internal discipline. *See* minutes of the negotiations of Working Group B of Committee 1.

Original Suit

Suit commenced in the first court. *See* RA(DSR), Para 534.

Other Devices

Manually emplaced munitions and devices including improvised explosive devices designed to kill, injure or damage and which are actually actuated manually, by remote control or automatically after a lapse of time. *See* Article 2.5 of the Protocol on Prohibitions or Restrictions on the Use of

Mines, Booby Traps and Other Devices as Amended on 3 May, 1996.

Other Punishments

These are:

(a) extra drill for two hours a day for 15 days,

(b) reduction to a lower class for pay for a period upto 28 days.

RA(DSR), para 443(b) read with Army Act, section 82.

OR

All combatants other than the officers, junior commissioned officers and warrant officers.

Other Trial

Another trial of a case in which the original proceedings were declared invalid because of lack of jurisdiction or failure of a charge to state an offence. [US RCM 810(e).]

Outlaw

Person who has forfeited the protection of law.

Outer Space

The space above air space.

See HPCR Draft Manual on Air and Missile Warfare.

Outlays

Actual expenditure.

Overpower

To vanquish by force, to subdue, to defeat.

Overrun

To ravage, to lay waste. A country which is harassed by incursions is said to be overrun.

Overstayal of Leave

Absence from duty by a military person for the period after expiry of his leave.

Overthrow

Total defeat, discomfiture, rout.

Owner of Property

The person in possession or control of property.

P

Pamphlet

A very thin book with a paper cover. *See* RA(DSR), para 612.

Para Military Forces

Forces or groups which are distinct from the regular armed forces of any country but which resemble them in organisation, equipment, training or mission such as the Border Security Force and Territorial Army. These are raised on military lines with the intent of supplementing the Armed Forces, both in peace and war. They function as an ancilliary to that of the military forces with leadership drawn from the Army or the Services. They are organised, equipped and trained on the pattern of the Army or the Services.

Pardon

It is an act of grace proceeding from the power which exempts the individual on whom it is bestowed from the punishment the law inflicts for a crime he has committed.

Parole

Release of a convict on parole may be granted by the Government on compassionate grounds where jail authorities so recommend and on advice of Army Headquarters. Release on parole with conditions suspends execution of the sentence.

Parties to Offences

Every person is a party to and guilty of an offence—

(a) who actually commits it;

(b) does or omits to do anything for the purpose of aiding any person to commit it;

(c) abets any person in committing it; or

(d) counsels or procures any person to commit it.

[Section 72(1) of the Canada's National Defence Act, 1985.]

Partnership

The term encompasses all relationships between a Movement component and a company, in which the Movement component grants the company the possibility of using its name, emblem/logo or image in its communication and promotional materials, thereby potentially creating a public association of image between the company and the Movement component. *See* Annex to Resolution 10 on Substantive Provisions of the International Red Cross and Red Crescent Movement Policy for Corporate Sector Partnership.

Pass

It is signification of a general permission to do certain things.

Passive Personality Principle

This principle of criminal jurisdiction determines jurisdiction by reference to the nationality or national character of the person injured by the offence.

Patrol

A detachment, sent out by a larger unit, for the purpose of securing or denying information or carrying out some special missions.

Pawn

To leave an object with a pawn broker in exchange for money. *See* Army Act, section 54(a).

Pay

It is the stipend or salary allowed for each individual serving in the Army, first established by British Government in the year 1660. For purposes of regulating traveling allowance (including daily allowance) under Travel Regulations, the term "Pay" includes in the case of Commissioned Officers, Basic Pay and Rank Pay wherever applicable and non-practicing allowance in case of medical officers.

Peace Building

Peace building covers actions, which support political, economic, social and military measures and structures aiming to strengthen solidify political settlements in order to redress the causes of conflict. This includes mechanisms to identify and support structures, which tend to consolidate peace, advance a sense of confidence and well-being and support economic reconstruction.

Peace Enforcement

Peace enforcement operations are undertaken under Chapter IV of the UN Charter. They are coercive in nature and are conducted when consent of all parties to a conflict has not been achieved or might be uncertain. They are designed to maintain or re-establish peace or enforce the terms specified in the mandate. It implies the use of force or its threat, to coerce hostile factions to cease and desist from violent action.

Peaceful Civilians

The term used in International Humanitarian Law in the context of direct participation in hostilities denotes civilians who at the relevant time do not "directly participate in the hostilities" and, therefore, are not subject to direct attack.

Peacekeeping

Peacekeeping aims to prevent convict, or its resumption, by the physical separation of hostile elements by a third party, to allow negotiations to reach a political settlement. The need to avoid the use of force, except as a last resort, gives peacekeeping a unique character. International peacekeeping may be carried out under the authority of the United Nations or on a regional basis. It is also defined as the deployment of a United Nations presence in the field, hitherto with the consent of all the parties concerned, normally involving United Nations Military and/or police personnel and frequently civilians as well. Peace keeping is a technique that expands the possibilities for both the prevention of conflict and the making of peace.

Peacekeeping Operations

Peacekeeping operations are generally undertaken under Chapter VI of the United Nations Charter and are conducted with the consent of all the parties to a conflict, to monitor and facilitate the implementation of a peace agreement. Operations are carried out with the consent of the belligerent parties, in support of efforts to achieve or maintain peace, in order to promote security and sustain life in areas of potential or actual conflict. These operations are not of a coercive nature but are based on the consensus of the sides in conflict in respect to which they assume an impartial role; moreover, in such operations the use of force is, as a rule, only allowed for legitimate defence.

Peacemaking

The diplomatic activities conducted after the commencement of a conflict aimed at establishing a cease-fire or a rapid peaceful settlement. They can include the provision of good offices, mediation, conciliation and such actions as diplomatic pressure, isolation or sanctions.

Peace Operations

Military operations to support diplomatic efforts to reach a long-term political settlement and categorised as peace keeping operations and peace enforcement operations.

Peace Support Operations

Multi-functional operations involving military forces and diplomatic and humanitarian agencies. They are designed to achieve humanitarian goals or long-term political settlement and are conducted impartially in support of an appropriate mandate. These include peacekeeping, peace enforcement, conflict prevention, and peacemaking, peace-building and humanitarian operations.

Pecuniary

Monetary, relating to money. *See* Army Act, section 2(xiv).

Penal Deductions

A penal deduction is, in principle, a deduction made as a penalty for an offence of which an accused has been convicted and constitutes part or the whole of this punishment. The term also means every deduction which is authorised in Army Act, sections 90, 91 and 95.

Penal Servitude

A punishment which consists in keeping an offender in confinement, and compelling him to labour.

Pending

Waiting to be decided or settled.

Pension

A stated allowance or stipend to a person in consideration of past services; a specified sum granted by Government to retired members of the Armed Forces who have served a certain number of years or have been wounded.

Perceives

To notice or become aware of something, to understand or think of somebody/something in a particular way. *See* Army Act, section 14.

Perfidy

Acts inviting the confidence of an adversary to lead it to believe that it is entitled to, or is obliged to accord, protection under the rules of international law applicable in armed conflict, with the intent to betray that confidence constitute perfidy. Perfidious acts include the launching of an attack while feigning:

(a) exempt, civilian, neutral or protected United Nations status;

(b) surrender or distress by, *e.g.*, sending a distress signal or by the crew taking to life rafts.

See Remo Manual.

Peril

Exposure to injury, loss or destruction. *See* Army Act, sections 17(2) and 34(1).

Perjury

Wilful *i.e.*, intentional giving of evidence which he knows to be false or does not believe to be true by a witness or interpreter in a judicial proceeding.

Permanent Disability

A patient is 'permanently disabled' or under a 'permanent disability' when his actual or presumed ability to engage in gainful activities stands reduced or absent because of 'impairment' and no fundamental or marked change in the future can be expected.

Permanent Duty

Any move on duty which, as per the expectation of the ordering authority, the individual shall do duty in the station to which his transfer is ordered for period exceeding 180 days. [Travel Regulations, para 56.]

"Permanent Medical Personnel", "Permanent Medical-Units" and "Permanent Medical Transports"

Those assigned exclusively to medical purposes for an indeterminate period. "Temporary medical personnel", "temporary medical-units" and "temporary medical transports" mean those devoted exclusively to medical purposes for limited periods during the whole of such periods. Unless otherwise specified, the terms "medical personnel", "medical-units" and "medical transports" cover both permanent and temporary categories.

[Article 8(k) – Protocol Additional to the Geneva Conventions of 12 August, 1949, and Relating to the Protection of Victims of International Armed Conflicts (Protocol I), 8 June, 1977.]

Permit

It is confined to permission to do a particular act.

Perpetrator

He is one who actually commits the offence, either by the perpetrator's own hand, or by causing an offence to be committed by knowingly or intentionally inducing or setting in motion acts by an animate or inanimate agency or instrumentality which results in the commission of an offence.

Persecution

Intentional and severe deprivation of fundamental rights contrary to international law by reason of the identity of the group or collectively. *See* Article 2.1(g) of the ICC Statute.

Persona Non Grata

A diplomatic representative unacceptable to the receiving State.

Personal Ethics

The set of beliefs about right and wrong, good and bad, morals and duties that originate from the individual.

Personal Equipment

All material issued to an officer or non-commissioned member for the personal wear or other personal use of that officer on non-commissioned officer. Section 2 of the Canada's National Defence Act, 1985.

Personal Interest

It is not limited to private interest but may well include official interest. *See* Army Rule 39(2)(e).

Personal Number

An individual number allotted to all officers including Territorial Army and National Cadet Corps Officers, Junior

Commissioned Officers and Warrant Officers for use in the Gazette of India, all official correspondence and documents etc. *See* RA(DSR), para 618.

Personation

The act of pretending to be a person. *See* RS(DSR), para 575.

Persons Attending the Trial

Two persons are required to attend a Summary Court-Martial throughout. They shall be officers or JCOs or one of either. They shall not be sworn or affirmed. [Army Act, section 116(2).]

Persuasive Precedent

The authority of judicial decisions which depends on their intrinsic value and not on their character as formal precedents.

Petty Officer

A sailor rated as such and includes a chief petty officer and a master chief petty officer. *See* Navy Act, section 3(17).

Photograph

Include still photographs, X-ray films, video tapes, and motion pictures. [US MRE 1001(2).]

Picket

A detachment dispatched to act as out guard; to act as a picket; a military punishment in the British Army as late as the 18th century. The offender was hung by the right waist from a high post, with his bare heel resting on a blunt pointed stake driven into the ground. It was finally abandoned as causing too much injury.

Pillage

The act of taking property or money by violence. Also referred to as plundering, ravaging or looting. These acts are punishable as a war crime.

Piracy

As defined in 1982 UNCLOS, it is an act that can only be committed on the high seas and for which universal jurisdiction applies (that is to say, any State can apprehend a private vessel, regardless of its flag State). Piracy consists of the following:—

(a) Any illegal acts of violence, detention or any act of depredation, committed for private ends by the crew or passengers of a private ship or private aircraft, and directed on the high seas against another ship or aircraft, or against persons or property on board such ship or aircraft.

(b) Any act of voluntary participation in the operation of a ship or of an aircraft with knowledge of facts making it a pirate ship or aircraft.

(c) Any act of inciting or intentionally facilitating an act described in (a) and (b) above.

Piratical Attack

An attack by a person on a ship at sea to other ship.

Place of Duty

Includes any place of duty, whether permanent or temporary, fixed or mobile. [US MCM IV-35.]

Plaint

A statement in writing of the cause of action in a suit. *See* RA(DSR), para 547.

Plea

A defence of matters of fact. That which is pleaded in justification or excuse, that which is demanded by pleading.

Plea Bargaining

Wherein criminal cases, the accused instead of defending his case in proper defence simply pleades guilty under a promise or assurance that he would be let off lightly.

Plea in Bar

An accused may offer a plea in bar on the ground that he has been previously convicted or acquitted of the offence by a criminal court or by a court-martial or has been punished or dealt with summarily for that offence, or a re-proof has been administered to him, or a charge in respect of the offence has been dismissed or that the offence has been pardoned or condoned by competent authority, or that the offence is time barred. *See* Army Rule 53(1)(a) and Notes thereto.

Plea of No Case

At the close of the case of the prosecution, the accused may offer a plea that the evidence given on behalf of the prosecution in respect of one or more charges has not established a *prima facie* case against him and that he should not, therefore, be called upon to make his defence to that charge or charges. *See* Army Rule 57.

Plea to Jurisdiction

It is a plea to the right to try the accused on any charge, as distinct from a plea which relates to a particular charge.

Plunder

To take property from persons or places by open force and this may be in the course of a lawful war or by unlawful hostility, as in the case of pirates or bandits. The term should be understood to embrace all forms of unlawful appropriation of property in armed conflict for which individual criminal responsibility attaches under international law, including those acts traditionally described as "pillage".

Plural Marriage

Refers to the situation where a person who has already solemnized or registered his/her marriage, remarries during the life time of his or her wife or husband. *See* RA(DSR), para 333.

Poison

A substance that causes illness or death if taken into a living thing, especially a person's or animal's body. Any substance which, when introduced into or absorbed by a living organism, destroys life or injures health; irrespective of mechanical means or direct thermal changes. Popularly applied to a substance capable of destroying life by rapid action, and when taken in a small quantity.

Possesses

To exercise control of something. Possession may be direct physical custody. Possession must be knowing and conscious. Possession inherently includes the power or authority to preclude control by others.

Possession

Under Canada's National Defence Act, 1985, a person has anything in possession when the person has it in the person's personal possession or knowingly:

(a) has it in the actual possession or custody of another person; or

(b) has it in any place, whether or not that place belongs to or is occupied by the person, for the use or benefit of the person or of another person; and

(c) where one of two or more persons, with the knowledge and consent of the rest, has anything in the person's custody or possession, it shall be deemed to be in the custody and possession of each and all of them.

Post

A soldier's beat while on sentry duty or a position assigned to or taken up by a soldier or body of men, a place where a soldier is stationed. Post includes any point or position (whether fortified or not) which a detachment may be ordered to hold; and the abandonment of a post would also include the abandonment of a seize. Note 3(c) to Army Act, section 34. On the other hand, when used with respect to an individual as in clause (h) and (k) of section 34 would mean the position or place in which it may be the duty of a person subject to the Army Act to be, especially when under arms with respect to a sentry, it applies (i) to the spot where the sentry is left to the observance of his duties by his officer, JCO or NCO posting him, or (ii) to any limit specially pointed out as his beat.

Post Connected With Defence

Posts which are auxiliary to or are directly related to or incidental to the tasks performable by the defence forces, or require performance of duties on which the effective functioning of the defence forces both in time of peace and war depends. See *J.M. Ajwani* v. *Union of India*, 1967 SLR 471 (SC).

Posting

Posting or transfer of officers within the regular Army is carried out under the orders of the Chief of the Army Staff.

RA(DSR), para 64. Posting is the term applied to the movement of a man from one part of his Corps to another part, as from one Battalion to another, or to the Depot, or the permanent staff of a Battalion of the Territorial Army; this can be done without the man's consent.

Postpone

Defer, put off, keep for a later time, adjourn. *See* Army Act, section 126(1).

Power

The ability to control people or things, the right or authority of a person or group to do something, strength or influence in a particular area of activity. *See* Army Rule 2(d).

Power of Superintendence

This power is not confined to administrative superintendence but includes the power of judicial revision also even when no appeal or revision lies under the ordinary law, courts or tribunals constituted by or under any law relating to the armed forces have been kept out of the power of superintendence of High Courts. [Constitution of India, Article 227(4).]

Preamble

Introductory part of a statute or treaty.

Precaution

Something that is done in advance in order to prevent problems or to avoid danger. *See* Army Act, section 35(a). The principle of precaution ordains that in the running of the military operations, each side in conflict will have to take, in compliance with the laws and obligations derived from the rules of international law applicable to armed conflicts, all reasonable precautions so as to avoid loss of life among the civilian population and damage to civilian property. *See* Article 57, IPA.

Precision

The quality of being exact, accurate and careful. *See* Army Act, section 135(4).

Pre-Confirmation

The entire military legal process undertaken after the finding and or sentence is announced by a court-martial and till the proceedings are confirmed by the confirming authority.

Preferential

Giving an advantage to a particular person or group. *See* RA(DSR), para 539.

Prejudice

An unreasonable dislike of or preference for a person, group, custom etc., without affecting any other legal matter. *See* Army Act, section 191(2).

Preliminary Investigation

Prior to the appearance before the commanding officer of an alleged offender, a preliminary investigation into his case is generally made by his squadron or company commander, or by corresponding officer in other branches of service. *See* MML, Vol. I, Chapter III, para 12 and RA(DSR), para 402(c).

Premature Retirement

Retirement prior to the age of superannuation. While permanent regular commissioned officers can avail premature retirement, this clause is not attracted in case of short service or women special entry commission. It is applicable to an officer eligible by length of service for pension or gratuity. *See* Army Rule 16B. Present policy makes this term applicable to only permanent commissioned officers who have rendered ten years of service or more, and are eligible for grant of pension or gratuity or both and who wish to retire prior to the date of superannuation.

Prescribed

Prescribed by Rules made under the Army Act. *See* Army Act, section 3(xix).

Preservation

The term is used in section 7B of the TA Act, 1948, in the context of continuation of rights over such provident fund or superannuation scheme for the benefit of employees with regard to a person required to perform military service.

Presiding Officer

At every general, district or summary general court-martial the senior member shall be the Presiding Officer. *See* Army Act, section 128. Similarly, the senior member of a court of inquiry is called the Presiding Officer.

Presumed

To suppose that something is true, although you do not have actual proof. *See* Army Rule 32(2).

Presumption

A supposition opinion, or belief previously formed. It is probable inference which common sense draws from circumstances usually occurring in such cases. *See* Army Rule 58(2). Presumptions are either of law or of fact, and when of law may be either conclusive or rebuttable.

Presumption of Innocence

Everyone shall be presumed innocent until proved guilty before the court in accordance with the applicable law. The *onus* is on the prosecutor to prove the guilt of the accused.

Pre-trial Agreement

An agreement between the accused and the convening authority, usually to limit the amount of punishment that can be imposed in a court-martial in return for a plea of guilty to some or all of the charges.

Pre-trial Allied Papers

These papers should include: (1) Advice of staff Judge Advocate or legal adviser; (2) requests by counsel and action of the convening authority taken thereon; (3) any other paper, endorsements, investigations which accompanied the charges when referred for trial; (4) record of any former trial.

Pre-trial Investigation

An investigation under Article 32, UCMJ that is required before convening a General Court-Martial.

Pre-trial Publicity

In the form of public comments on the guilt of an accused which threaten the impartiality of court members down the chain of command on a special problem, albeit infrequent, with command influence.

Primacy

The fact of being the most important person or thing.

Prima Facie Case

A case made out by proper and sufficient testimony, one which is established by sufficient evidence.

Primary Evidence

Primary evidence means the document itself produced for inspection of court. *See* IEA, section 62.

Principle of Unnecessary Suffering

It is strictly forbidden to employ arms, projectiles or material calculated to cause unnecessary suffering. This principle applies to legality of weapons.

Prisoner of War

Persons as defined in the Geneva Convention relative to the treatment of prisoner of war (August 12, 1949, Part I, Article 4); those of the enemy who are taken in or after a battle; seize etc. They are deprived of their liberty at large, until exchanged, or sent on parole.

Prisoner of War Cage

A temporary construction, building or enclosed area, to which prisoners of war are evacuated for interrogation and temporary detention pending further evacuation.

Prisoner of War Camps

A camp of a semi permanent nature established in the communication zone or zone of interior (home country) for the internment and complete administration of prisoners of war. It may be located on or independent of, other military installations.

Prisoner of War Collecting Point

A designated locality in a front line area where prisoners are assembled pending local examination for information of immediate tactical value and subsequent evacuation.

Prisons, Military

Places of confinement for soldiers undergoing long sentences by court-martial.

Privilege

A special right or advantage that a particular person or group of people has. *See* Army Act, section 31.

Privy

Secretly cognizant, privately knowing, admitted to the participation of knowledge with another of a secret transaction. *See* Army Act, section 57(a).

Procedure

A series of related tasks that make up the chronological sequence and the established way of performing the work to be accomplished.

Proceeds

Any funds derived from or obtained, directly or indirectly, through the commission of an offence set forth in Article 4. *See* Additional Protocol to the SAARC Regional Convention on Suppression of Terrorism, Islamabad, 6 January, 2004.

Proceeds of Crime

Shall mean any property derived from or obtained directly or indirectly, through the commission of an offence. *See* Article 2(e) of the United Nations Convention Against Transnational Organised Crime.

Proceeds of Terrorism

All kinds of properties which have been derived or obtained from commission of any terrorist act or have been acquired through funds traceable to a terrorist act, and shall include cash, irrespective of person in whose name such proceeds are standing or in whose possession they are found.

Proclamation

The act of publishing orders; conspicuous announcement.

Procurement

Act of buying goods and services for the Government.

Producing Disease

To produce disease is willfully to cause genuine disease to develop, *e.g.*, by the infection of microbes or poisonous drugs. *See* Note 8 to Army Act, section 46.

Professional Ethics

The standards and rules that govern the conduct of all members of a specific profession.

Prohibited Means of Warfare

Include various kinds of weapons of indiscriminate character and/or those that cause unnecessary suffering:

(a) bullets that expand or flatten easily in the human body;

(b) projectiles used with the only purpose to spread asphyxiating or poisonous gases;

(c) projectiles weighing less than 400 gms, which are either explosive or charged with fulminating or inflammable substances;

(d) poisons or poisoned weapons;

(e) asphyxiating, poisonous or other similar gases and bacteriological means;

(f) bacteriological (biological) and toxin weapons;

(g) environmental modification techniques having widespread, long term or serious effects as means of destruction, damage or injury.

Prohibition

The act of stopping something being done or used. *See* Army Act, section 121.

Prolongation of Service

The detention of a soldier in army service for any period, not exceeding twelve months, after the date at which he would be entitled to be transferred to the Reserve or discharged. A soldier's service may be thus prolonged by the competent Military Authority, when—(i) A state of war exists; (ii) He is on service out of the country; (iii) The Reserves are called out.

Promise

Engagement for the performance or non-performance of some particular thing, a declaration made to another person with respect to the future. *See* Army Act, section 17(2).

Promulgation

It is reading out to the accused of the charge, finding, sentence, any recommendations to mercy and confirmation or non confirmation of the proceedings. Right of accused to submit a petition is also explained to him. Fact of promulgation is recorded in court-martial proceedings below the confirmation minute.

Proof

Conclusive evidence.

Proper Military Authority

When used in relation to any power, duty, act, or matter, such military authority as, in pursuance of these rules or the regulations made under the Act or the usages of the service, exercises or performs that power or duty or is concerned with the act or matter. *See* Army Rule 2(d).

Proportionality

The principle of proportionality prohibits attacks "which may be expected to cause incidental loss of civilian life, injury to civilians, damage to civilian objects or a combination thereof, which would be excessive in relation to the concrete and direct military advantage anticipated" from the operations. Section AP I Article 51.5(b) note 29 and Article 57.2. The anticipated loss of life and damage to property incidental to attacks must not be excessive in relation to the concrete and direct military advantage expected to be gained.

Proposition

An idea or plan of action that is suggested, a suggested change to the law that people can note on that which is propounded. *See* Army Rule 32(2).

Propriety

The rules of correct behaviour. *See* Army Act, section 164(1).

Prosecute

To charge a person with a crime and thereafter pursue the case through trial on behalf of the government.

Prosecutor

On a court-martial, the person who originates the charge; the prisoner's commanding officer, or a staff officer, may be ordered to perform the duty, in inferior courts the adjutant of the prisoner's regiment is usually the prosecutor.

Prospective

Potential, expected to happen soon, forthcoming. *See* Army Rule 20.

Protected Persons

Are those who, at a given moment and in any manner, whatsoever, find themselves, in case of a conflict or occupation, in the hands of a Party to the conflict or occupying power of which they are not nationals. Article 4(1), GC IV. The term applies to anyone who, on the basis of the Geneva Conventions and their Additional Protocols, has the right to special protection, *i.e.*, to special protected status.

Protecting Power

A neutral or other state, not a Party to the conflict which has been designated by a Party to the conflict, and accepted by the adverse Party and has agreed to carry out the functions assigned to a Protecting Power under the Conventions and Additional Protocol 1.

Protection

Immunity from protection granted to some class of persons such as army personnel acting in furtherance of duties performed while provisions of Armed Forces (Special Powers) Act are invoked.

Protective Personality Principle

A nation may also have the authority to establish and enforce criminal laws regarding conduct abroad which injures one of its nationals. Although perhaps not yet reflective of customary international law, this principle has gained increasing recognition in cases involving international terrorism.

Protective Principle

This principle of criminal jurisdiction determines jurisdiction by reference to the national interest injured by the offence. In the context of fight against international terrorism, it implies that a nation has the authority to establish and enforce criminal laws regarding conduct outside its territory that threatens its security, so long as that conduct is generally recognised as criminal by State in international community.

Protest

Statement of dissent or disapproval.

Protocol

The first or original version of an agreement, especially a treaty between countries, etc; an extra part added to an agreement or treaty.

Provincial Unit

A unit having training annually in camp. *See* Rule 2(g) of the Territorial Army Rules, 1948.

Provost Marshal

A functionary appointed for the prompt and instant repression of irregularities and offences committed in the field; or on the march and vested with powers of a special and extraordinary nature; the offspring of the exigencies of armies in the field.

Public Authority

The Central Government or a State Government or a local authority; and, so far as regards tolls levied by a railway company under section 4 of the Indian Guaranteed Railways Act, 1879, or section 51 of the Indian Railways Act, 1930, includes such a railway company.

Public Claim

Any public debt or disallowances including any over issue; or a deficiency or irregular expenditure of public money or store of which, after due investigation no explanation satisfactory to the Central Government is given by the person who is responsible for the same. *See* Army Rule 205.

Public Condemnation

A public statement by the ICRC to the effect that acts which can be attributed to a party to or conflict—whether or not they are known to the public—constitute a violation of international humanitarian law.

Public Domain

Domain that has no restrictions upon dissemination of information within or from it; the existence of any legal rights to intellectual property in that information does not remove such information from being in public domain.

See section 4(i) of the Weapons of Mass Destruction and Their Delivery Systems (Prohibition of Unlawful Activities) Act, 2005.

Public Funds

Include all funds which are financed entirely from public money, the unexpended balances of which are refundable to Government in the event of not being devoted to the objects for which granted, and also—(i) unused pay and allowances; (ii) office allowance fund; and (iii) the estates of deceased men and deserters. *See* RA(DSR), para 801.

Public Money

The term refers to the revenue or assets through which public funds are financed.

Public Order

The concept is synonymous with public peace, safety and tranquility. See *Superintendent, Central Prison* v. *Ram Manohar Lohia,* AIR 1960 SC 633.

Public Place

Any place which is open to the use and enjoyment of the public, whether it is actually used or enjoyed by the public or not. *See* section 2(xxxi) of the Cantonment Act, 1924.

Public Prosecutor

A public official charged with the investigation and prosecution of punishable acts on behalf of a State or international commission. *See* RA(DSR), para 542.

Public Utility Service

Any undertaking which supplies power, light, gas or water to the public or carries on a public transport, or maintains any system of public conservancy or sanitation and which is declared by notification in the Official Gazette, by the Central Government to be a public utility service to which Territorial Army Act applies. *See* section 2(dd) of the said Act.

Publicly

To tell people about something that is secret. *See* Army Rule 20.

Punishments, Military

Sentences awarded by courts-martial or commanding officers for crimes committed by officers or soldiers. They are detailed in the Articles of war/Army Acts.

Punitive Articles

Articles 77 through 134 of the UCMJ. These articles generally describe various crimes and state how they may be punished.

Purporting

This expression means that if a paper appears to be certified or to be signed as mentioned therein, it can be accepted without calling a witness to prove that it has been so certified, signed etc., unless indeed some evidence is given to the contrary.

Q

Qualifying Service

The Pension Regulations mandate that the qualifying service of an officer is assessed in accordance with Regulation 26 (regulation 37 in the case of officers of the Military Nursing Service) for the purpose of service element of the disability pension and in accordance with regulation 27(regulation 38 in the case of officers of the Military Nursing Service) for the purpose of a final gratuity. Service rendered in aid of the civil power shall be treated as military service for the purpose of disability pension and final gratuity.

Pension Regulations for the Army, 1961, Part I, para 58.

Quality Assurance

A planned and systematic pattern of all actions necessary to provide confidence that adequate technical requirements are established, that products and services conform to established technical requirements, and that satisfactory performance is achieved.

Quarter Guard

A small guard mounted in camp, posted in the front of each battalion or unit. It is placed in front of the centre of the camp, at about 80 paces from it.

Quits

Goes, absent without authority.

R

Ragging

It implies an act of teasing, tormenting, playing rough jokes on someone or engaging in rough play, adversely affecting the individual mentally or physically.

Raid

An operation, usually small scale, involving a swift penetration of hostile territory to secure information, confuse the enemy or destroy his installations/headquarters. It ends with a planned withdrawal on completion of the assigned task.

Rank

The relative position in the Army which officers and men hold with respect to each other; the grade or status of relative precedence in the armed services held by a person by virtue of a commission, warrant, appointment etc. which empower him to exercise authority or command over other persons.

Rank Pay

The pay admissible to an officer appropriate to the rank actually held, either in acting or substantive capacity, in addition to the pay in the revised scale. Rank pay forms part of the basic pay. *See* Special Army Instructions 2/S/1998.

Rating

The name (such as "boatswain's mate") prescribed for members of an armed force in an occupational field. "Rate" means the name (such as "chief boatswain's mate") prescribed for members on the same rating or other category who are in the same grade (such as Chief Petty Officer or seaman apprentice).

Readily

Quickly and without difficulty. *See* Army Rule 23(5).

Real Evidence

This refers to physical objects such as chattels, persons, animals or objects with an inscription or words thereon which may be produced for inspection by the court.

Reasonable Care

Such care as a person of ordinary prudence would take. Reasonable care and prudence implies the converse of negligence.

Reasonable Doubt

An honest misgiving generated by the insufficiency of proof. Such a doubt as honest, conscientious painstaking men may entertain upon a state of facts presented to them.

Reasonable Grounds

There must be that kind of reliable information that a reasonable, prudent person would rely on, which makes it more likely than not that something is true.

Reasonable Suspicion

The amount of knowledge about the suspected criminal sufficient to induce an ordinary prudent and cautious man to believe that a criminal act was going to be committed.

Reasoned Finding

A finding expressly supported by reasons. Giving of reasons in support of an order or finding is one of the principles of natural justice which mandates that a party has the right to know not only the conclusion drawn in the inquiry or trial but also the reasons as to how or on what basis said conclusion has been drawn.

Rebels

One who opposed authority or restraint; one who breaks with established customs or traditions. *See* Army Act, section 2(x).

Rebut

To say or prove that a statement or criticism is false, refute. *See* Army Rule 64(3).

Receipt

A voucher or acknowledgement, which should always be given when official papers or stores or funds are received.

Receiving

The offence of receiving is committed by a person subject to military law who receives any property knowing it to have been so stolen. A person who receives goods with knowledge that they have been stolen or obtained by another in any way whatsoever under circumstances which amount to felony or misdeameanour, commits the offence of receiving.

Reciprocity

Identity or, at least, equivalence of rights and duties.

Reckless

The operation or physical control of a vehicle, vessel, or aircraft is reckless when it exhibits a culpable disregard of foreseeable consequences to others from the act or omission involved.

Recklessness

Generally consists of the state of mind of a person who does not intend to cause a harmful result but takes an unjustifiable risk of which he is aware, thus causing an unlawful result.

Recognised Suspicion

The word 'recognised' must be understood to refer to norms contained in human rights treaties, norms that form part of international customary law, or norms that form part of principles of law as recognised by civilised nations.

Recommendation

An official suggestion about the best thing to do; an expression of opinion. *See* Army Rules 13 and 66.

Recommendation to Mercy

The court-martial may, in awarding sentence, make a recommendation to mercy. If such recommendation is made, it must form part of the proceedings and the reason for it must be recorded. *See* Army Rule 66.

Reconsideration

Taking up for renewed consideration that which has been acted on or decided previously. *See* Army Act, section 187.

Recordable

This term is used in relation to censures awarded by senior commanders which are preserved by committing to writing in the dossiers of the individuals concerned.

Recording

A physical, administrative and technical operation designed to obtain, for the purpose of registration in official records, all available information facilitating the location of minefields, mines, booby-traps and other devices. *See* Article 2 of Protocol on Prohibitions or Restrictions on the Use of Mines, Booby-Traps and Other Devices as Amended on 3 May, 1996.

Recover

To get back or find something that was lost, stolen or missing. *See* Army Act, section 29(2).

Recreational

Connected with activities that people do for enjoyment when they are not working. *See* Army Rule 19.

Recruit

To enlist new soldiers, to get or seek fresh supplies of men for the army, to persuade someone to become a new member of an organisation especially the army.

Redress

To correct something that is unfair or wrong. *See* Army Act, section 27.

Reduction

An act of making something less or smaller, the state of being made less or smaller.

Re-engage

A soldier may, after specified year's service, be permitted to re-engage to complete a total of say twenty-one year's army service, under such regulations as may be made by the Army Council. Such soldier must sign re-engagement paper.

Re-enlist

To enlist again.

Re-examination

After cross-examination, the party which called the witness may re-examine him. Such re-examination must be directed to explanation of matters referred to in cross-examination. Leading questions can not be asked.

Referral

It is the order of a convening authority that charges against an accused will be tried by a specified court-martial.

[US RCM 601(a).]

Refugee

Is as a result of events occurring before 1 January, 1951, and owing to well-founded fear of being persecuted for reasons of race, religion, nationality, membership of a particular social group or political opinion, is outside the country of his (or her) nationality and is unstable, or owing to such fear, is unwilling to avail himself (or herself) of the protection of that country; or who, or having a nationality and being outside the country of his (or her) former habitual residence as a result of such events, is unable, or owing to such fear, is unwilling to return to it. [Article 1A(2)].

Refugee Law

Its provisions apply whenever a person flees his homeland seeking protection in another country out of justified fear of persecution.

Regiment

In all modern armies, is a Colonel's Command and the largest permanent association of soldiers. In the regiment, the same officers serve continually and in command of the same body of men.

Regimental

The expression means connected with a corps, or with any battalion or other sub-division of a corps.

Regimental Claim

When a person subject to Army Act does not accept his liability in respect of regimental dues, it becomes a regimental claim. *See* Army Rule 205.

Regimental Debt

When a person subject to Army Act accepts his liability in respect of regimental dues, it becomes a regimental debt. *See* Note 1 to Army Rule 205.

Regimental Duty

All employment with units of own Arms or Service, service with other Arms or Services when filling appointments tenable by personnel of own Arms or Service, period spent on authorised courses as students except at institutions training solely for employment on staff, and service with the Territorial Army when embodied. *See* RA(DSR) – explanation of terms used.

Regimental Funds

These comprise all funds other than public funds as defined in RA(DSR), para 801 maintained by units, formations and Army Headquarters.

Regional War

Limited wars arising out of regional issues.

Registrant

A person applying with registration fee to the Organisation for booking of a dwelling unit under these Rules, and his application having been accepted. *See* AWHO Master Brochure, July 1987.

Registration

Making entries in the organisation's records of an application duly received, checked and accepted and given a registration number. *See* AWHO Master Brochure, July 1987.

Regular Army

Officers, junior commissioned officers, warrant officers, non-commissioned officers and other enrolled persons who by their commission, warrant, terms of enrolment or otherwise are liable to render continuously for a term military service to the Union in any part of the world, including persons belonging to the Reserve Forces and the Territorial Army when called out on permanent service. *See* Army Act, section 3(xxi).

Regular Forces

Officers and soldiers who by their commission, terms of enlistment, or otherwise, are liable to render continuously for a term military service to the State in every part of the world, or in any specified part of the world, including soldiers of the reserve forces when called out on permanent service, and including, subject to the modifications, Marines. The distinction between regular and other forces is that the regular forces are liable to serve continuously in any part of the world, or in any specified part of the world.

Regulation

The word includes a regulation made under the Army Act. *See* Army Act, section 3(xxii).

Reimbursements

Amounts received by an activity for the cost of material, work or services furnished to others, for credit to an appropriation or their fund account.

Reinstate

The term is used in the context of duty of every employer to take the person back in his employment on the termination of military service in an occupation and under conditions not less favourable to him prior to the interruption. *See* section 7A of the TA Act, 1948.

Rejoinder

In military law, the defendant's answer to the plaintiff's replication. The weight of the authority is against permitting a rejoinder on the part of the prisoner, unless evidence has been adduced in reply of the prosecutor. But such evidence should not be permitted in reply, and there should be no rejoinder.

Release

To let somebody or something come out of a place where they have been kept *e.g.*, release of a person from military service or release of a prisoner or convict from custody. Under section 2 of the Canada's National Defence Act, 1985, the term means the termination of service of an officer or non-commissioned officer in any manner.

Released Army Personnel

Refers to army personnel who have been separated from their service liability by having been released.

Release from Arrest

The release of a person under arrest may be ordered by the officer who imposed the arrest or the superior to whom it may have been reported, but as a rule, except in cases of obvious error, the release should not be ordered without the sanction of the highest authority to whom the case may have been referred. *See* RA(DSR), para 394.

Release Medical Board

It is held once the decision to discharge a person is taken and date of discharge is fixed. It is not only for the persons who are discharged on medical grounds but also for those who are released, retired and who complete their tenure. It is held to assess the percentage of disability of a person and give its opinion with regard to the attributability and aggravation of a disease or disability due to army service.

Relegation

To give somebody a lower or less important position, rank etc. than before. To relegate in the military academies for a cadet would mean to come down to a lower term.

Relevant Activity

Means,—

(i) the development, production, handling, operation, maintenance, storage, or dissemination of a nuclear, chemical or biological weapon; or

(ii) the development, production, maintenance, storage or dissemination of missiles specially designed for delivering any such weapon.

See section 4(j) of the Weapons of Mass Destruction and their Delivery Systems (Prohibition of Unlawful Activities) Act, 2005.

Relief

An order, given by the Minister of War, to authorise an officer to receive the arrears of pay which had accumulated during his absence from the Regiment.

Relieved

To replace somebody who is on duty, to free or clear from an obligation. *See* Army Act, section 34(h).

Religious Personnel

Military or civilian persons, such as chaplains, who are exclusively engaged in the work of their ministry and attached:

(a) to the armed forces of a Party to the conflict;

(b) to medical units or medical transports of a Party to the conflict;

(c) to medical units or medical transports described in Article 9, paragraph 2; or

(d) to civil defence organizations of a Party to the conflict.

The attachment of religious personnel may be either permanent or temporary, and the relevant provisions mentioned under sub-paragraph(k) apply to them.

[Article 8(d) – Protocol Additional to the Geneva Conventions of 12 August, 1949, and Relating to the Protection of Victims of International Armed Conflicts (Protocol I), 8 June, 1977.]

Remand

The process for a commanding officer to arrive at a decision whether or not to send a case for trial of an offender by court-martial. *See* Army Rule 24 and Army Act, section 120(2). To send back as when a soldier who has been discharged from prison or the guard house for the purpose of being examined or tried is sent back to await the final decision of his case.

Remedy

As a legal term means to enforce a right, a mode prescribed by law to enforce a duty or redress a wrong; that which gives relief to the party aggrieved.

Remembrancer

An officer of the judiciary responsible for collecting debts.

Remission

May be remission of the whole or part of the sentence, thus a sentence of imprisonment may be remitted altogether, or a portion of the term may be remitted. This term is also used for providing relief with regard to any forfeiture of pay and allowances. *See* Army Act, section 97 and Army Rule 195. Under UCMJ, an action by proper authority interrupting the execution of a punishment and cancelling out the punishment remaining to be served.

Remit

To lessen; as, to remit a part of a soldier's sentence.

Remittance

A sum of money that is sent to somebody in order to pay for something. *See* RA(DSR), para 533.

Remonstrate

To make a representation of a case or cases wherein one or more may consider themselves to be aggrieved.

Remote Control

Controls by commands from a distance. *See* Article 2 of the Protocol on Prohibitions or Restrictions on the Use of Mines, Booby-Traps and Other Devices as Amended on 3 May, 1996.

Removal

The act of taking somebody or something away from a particular place *e.g.*, removal of a person from military service.

Remuneration

Payment for services rendered or work done. *See* RA(DSR), para 831.

Reparation

Redressal of an illegal act.

Reply

It is the duty of a court to prevent new matter from being introduced into the prosecution or defence but an accused may urge in his defence mitigating circumstances, or examine witnesses as to character or services, and produce testimonials of such facts, without its being considered new matter. If any point of law is raised, the Judge Advocate may explain.

Report

Refers to a confidential report, adverse report, review report, interim confidential report or special report.

Report on Trial

Is the report issued by an officer of the Judge Advocate General's Department on the conclusion of any court-martial other than summary court-martial.

Representation of the Accused

At a trial by court-martial, the accused may represent himself or he may be represented by a defending officer or counsel.

Reprimand

A rebuke which is included in the military under the head of a minor punishment. It may take the form of a simple or severe reprimand and may be administered privately or publicly. May be given without the process of court-martial. One of the punishments provided for under the Army Act in the case of officers. May take the form either 'reprimand' or 'severe reprimand'. May be awarded by a court-martial or by an authority empowered to carry out summary disposal. It is a formal and public stigmatisation of an offence. In earlier times, it was a slighter kind of punishment sometimes inflicted on officers and non-commissioned officers. It consisted in reproving or reprimanding them at the head of their respective regiments, troop or company as was the case. A reprimand was then sometimes inserted in the orderly books.

Reprieve

The taking back or suspending a prisoner from the execution and proceedings of law for the time. It signifies the suspension for a time of the execution on a sentence which has been pronounced. It is the temporary suspension of the execution of a sentence, especially the sentence of death. *See* RA(DSR), para 583.

Reprisal

The taking one thing in satisfaction for another. Seizures in retaliation. Reprisals are conduct which otherwise would be unlawful, resorted to by one belligerent against enemy personnel or property for acts of warfare committed by the other belligerent in violation of the law of war, for the sole purpose of enforcing future compliance with the law of war.

Reproof

It is an administrative action for a minor offence or lapse. It may be verbal or written or both. It may just be a non-recordable 'Warning' by CO or a higher authority. *See* RA(DSR), para 327.

Reputation

Credit, honour, character, good name. The opinion that people have about what somebody/something is like, based on what has happened in the past. *See* RA(DSR), para 518.

Request for Information

These are issued by Service Headquarters where they are not certain of the specification of a system, in order to formulate realistic service qualitative requirements.

Request for Proposal

A self contained document to enable the vendors to make their offer after consideration of full requirements of the acquisition.

Requisition

A formal, official written request or demand for something. *See* RA(DSR), para 549.

Reservation

A keeping aside, the act of reserving or the fact of being reserved. *See* Army Act, section 8(2).

Reserve

With respect to an enlistment, appointment, grade or office means enlistment, appointment, grade, or office held as a reserve of an armed force.

Reserve Liability

On retirement from the Army with a pension or gratuity, regular officers are transferred to the Regular Reserve of officers. They are liable to be called up for service up to attaining the specified ages.

Reserve Forces

The Reserve Forces of the Army are composed of JCOs, NCOs and sepoys of all arms and services (including *Gorkhas*) transferred by virtue of their reserve liability. *See* RA(DSR), para 202. The term means the Army Reserve, including the Militia.

Reservist

Reservists are civilians performing part time military duty with military reserve or national guard units. They carry a liability to be recalled to active military service on mobilization. They may be inactive or active. Inactive (non-pay, non-duty) reservists are former active duty officers, enlistees and draftees waiting for their term of obligation to expire. The active reservist's basic obligations are to perform week end or short-term military duties.

Resident

Dwelling or having abode in any place, living, inhabitating, abiding. As a noun, a dweller or one who resides permanently in a place. *See* Army Act, section 64(f).

Resignation

The term is applicable to an officer leaving the Army before he becomes eligible by length of service for pension/gratuity or when an officer voluntarily resigns irrespective of the length of his service. *See* Army Rule 16C.

Resists

To oppose, to prevent, to hinder, to oppose with force. *See* Army Act, section 42(c).

Resolution

A formal statement of an opinion agreed on by a committee or a council, especially by means of a vote.

Responsibility

Subjects of international law must make reparation for their own illegal acts.

Responsibility

Is the obligation of a person to carry out the assignments and functions given to him by a person of higher authority.

Responsible

Being able to be blamed for something, to have to report to somebody/something with authority or in a higher position and explain to them what you have done. *See* Army Act, section 89(1).

Restoration

To give back, to make return or restitution. *See* RA(DSR), para 709.

Restraint

The act of controlling or limiting something because it is necessary or sensible to do so. *See* Army Act, section 172.

Restriction

It is the moral restraint of a person imposed by an order directing a person to remain within certain specified limits. It is also a form of non-judicial punishment awarded to the cadets in training academies. *See* Army Act, section 8(2).

Restriction in Lieu of Arrest

Under the UCMJ, it means moral restraint, less severe than arrest.

Retain

To continue to hold or contain something, to keep something, to continue to have something. *See* Army Rule 13.

Retaliation

Defined as infliction upon a wrongdoer of the same injury which he has caused another. This should never be resorted to as a measure of mere revenge, but only as a means of protective retribution, and more over, cautiously and unavoidably after careful inquiry into the real occurrence and the character of the misdeeds that may demand retribution.

Retarded Promotion

The term is used with regard to promotion of officers who fail to pass the prescribed professional examination within the time allowed leading to their promotions being retarded. *See* RA(DSR), para 71.

Retired List

Is a list of officers retired from the Army, Navy or Air Force.

Retirement

To withdraw from office, generally on superannuation; the act of retiring. It refers to the case of an officer eligible for retired pay or gratuity.

Retorsion

Legal, but unfriendly, acts in retaliation against acts of the same character.

Re-transfer

Transfer of any item notified under this Act from any country or entity to which it has been exported from India, to yet another country or entity.

See section 4(k) of the The Weapons of Mass Destruction and their Delivery Systems (Prohibition of Unlawful Activities) Act, 2005.

Re-trial

This should only be ordered in very exceptional circumstances, *e.g.*, where the court was illegally constituted, if it is highly undesirable, in the interests of discipline, that the accused should escape without punishment. *See* para 209 of Notes on Indian Military And Air Force Law.

Retroactive Effect

In accordance with the intention of the parties concerned, legal acts may date back to a time prior to such acts.

Retrospective

Intended to take effect from a particular date in the past rather than from the present date. *See* Army Rule 18.

Review

A review is a proceeding which exists by virtue of statute. It is in its nature a new trial of the issue previously tried between the parties, the cause of action being brought into court again for a trial by a new petition.

Revise

The power to revise includes the power to re-examine for correction, to alter or amend.

Revised Scale

In relation to officers of all Arms and Services including MNS officers, means the respective pay scale of that rank, whether fixed or otherwise specified against each rank in paragraph 3 of Army Instruction 2/S/1998.

Revision

A re-examination for correction. Where an officer who convenes a court-martial does not approve their proceedings, he may, under the Army Act, return them to the court for revision. Additional evidence may only be taken, if so indicated in the revision order.

Revolt

To renounce allegiance or subjection; to rise against the Government in declared rebellion.

Revolving Fund

A fund established to finance a cycle of operations to which reimbursements and collections are returned for reuse in a manner that will maintain the principal of the fund; *e.g.*, working capital funds and industrial funds.

Reward

A recompense given for good service. Rewards are either honorary or pecuniary.

Right of Private Defence

This is set out in IPC, sections 96 to 106. In brief, every person is entitled to defend his body or body of any other person, against any offence affecting the human body as also his property or property of any other person against theft, robbery, mischief or criminal trespass or attempts thereof. This right extends to the causing of death, grievous hurt, rape, unnatural offence, kidnapping, abduction or of wrongful confinement. It also extends to causing of death against offences (or attempts thereof) of robbery, house breaking by night, mischief by fire to a building, tent or vessel used as a human dwelling or for custody of property, or of theft, mischief or house trespass causing apprehension of death or grievous hurt. It is restricted to causing only as much harm as is necessary for the purpose of defence.

Right to Grieve

Under Canada's National Defence Act, 1985, an officer or non-commissioned member who has been aggrieved by any decision, act or omission in the administration of affairs of the

Canadian Forces for which no other process for redress is provided under the said Act is entitled to submit a grievance.

Ring Leader

The leader of a ring; especially, the leader of an association of men engaged in violation of law or an illegal enterprise, as rioters, mutineers, and the like.

Riot

When force or violence is used by an unlawful assembly or by any member thereof, in prosecution of the common object of such assembly, it becomes a riot. *See* IPC, section 146. It is a tumultuous disturbance of the peace by three or more persons assembled together in furtherance of a common purpose to execute some enterprise of a private nature by concerted action against anyone who might oppose them, committed in such a violent and turbulent manner as to cause or be calculated to cause public terror.

Robbery

It is an aggravated form of stealing from the person accompanied by violence or threats of injury to the person robbed or to his property.

Roll Call

For the sake of discipline and to prevent soldiers from wandering about indiscriminately at all hours, as well as for the purposes of having them available at any moment in case their services are required, the men of a regiment etc. should be present to answer their names during certain fixed periods of the day or at any time the Commanding Officer may think advisable.

Roll, Size

Is a list containing the names of all the men belonging to a troop or company, with the height or stature of each specifically marked.

Rout

It is an unlawful assembly which has made a motion towards the execution of the common purpose.

Royal Warrants

These were made by the King under the Royal Sign Manual and countersigned by the Secretary of State.

Rules of Engagement

Directives issued by the competent superior authority that delineate the circumstances and limitations under which forces will initiate and/or continue engagement with other forces encountered. These are orders issued to a military force by the chain of command that defines when and where they may initiate or continue to use force, and how much force may be used. They sometimes also define who within the chain of command is authorised to decide when force may be used. Operative orders given to the forces in the field to employ force legitimately and in compliance with the tasks undertaken at international level. Also defined as the directives issued by the competent military authority which specify the circumstances and the limitations under which the forces may initiate or continue combat with opposing forces.

Rules of Evidence

The rules whereby questions of fact are determined for judicial purposes.

Rules of Procedure

These were made, and when made, altered and repealed by the King, through a Secretary of State, under the Authority of the Army Act of the UK. These Rules must not contain anything contrary or inconsistent with the Act; but on any point as to which the Act is silent, any provision in the Rules has statutory force.

Running Amok

The situation when an armed solider has broken loose and is at large threatening or purporting to kill any one in particular or all or any in general. For provisions to deal with the situation, *see* RA(DSR), para 351.

Running Away

An unauthorised departure to avoid actual or impending combat. It need not, however, be the result of fear and there is no requirement that the accused literally ran. [United States Manual For Courts Martial (2000 edn) IV-35.]

Ruses of War

Stratagems of war. Any scheme or plan for deceiving and surprising an enemy. These are measures taken to obtain advantage of the enemy by mystifying or misleading him.

S

Sabotage

It is covert act, causing physical damage to property and equipment with a view to assist the enemy or a hostile foreign power for furthering a subversive political aim. *See* RA(DSR), para 599.

Safe Conduct

It is a document given by a commander of belligerent forces to enemy subjects or others authorising them, during a limited or unlimited period, to go into places which they could not reach without coming into collision with armed forces actively operating against the enemy – for instance, to visit or leave a besieged town.

Safeguard

A party of soldiers detached for the protection of some person or persons, or of a particular village, house or other property. A single sentry posted from such property is still part of the safeguard. *See* Note 2 to Army Act, section 36. A man posted to control traffic is not a safeguard. Some authorities say this term includes a written document, given to the person to be protected, or posted on the property itself.

Sailor

A person in the naval service other than an officer. *See* Navy Act, section 3(20).

Sanction

Of enforcing legal obligations. An official order that limits trade, contract etc, with a particular country, in order to make it to do something, such as obeying international law.

Satisfactory

Good enough for a particular purpose, acceptable. *See* Army Act, section 90(a).

Scale of Punishments

Army Act, sections 71 to 75 provide a scale of punishments which can be awarded by court-martial to a person subject to the Army Act. Also see RA(DSR), para 448.

Scandalous Conduct

The conduct which is not only prejudicial to good order and military discipline, but reflects such discredit upon the service that the offender is unfit to remain connected with it.

Scope

Aim, purpose, extent, limit etc. *See* Army Act, section 189.

Sealed Bidding

Replaces "formal advertising" in the contracting process in title only; the process remaining the same.

Seaman

Seaman means a person in the Naval organisation of India other than an officer. *See Union of India* v. *Jain R.C.*, 1984(1) SLR 591.

Search Warrant

It is an express permission to search and seize issued by competent civilian authority. [US MRE 315(2).]

Seating of Members

At a court-martial the members take their seat according to their Army rank. [Army Rule 75]. Further, it is laid down that members will take their seat according to their rank and seniority. [Special Army Order 1/S/2002/DV.]

Secondary Appropriation

An appropriation account increased as a result of reimbursable orders from an implementing agency which cites one of the implementing agency's appropriation accounts. Activity in a secondary appropriation is not categorised as Foreign Military Sales reimbursable.

Secondary Evidence

Copies or oral accounts of documents in circumstances specified in section 63 of IEA. Secondary evidence is that which is inferior to primary. Thus, a copy of an instrument or oral evidence of its contents is secondary evidence of the instrument and its contents. It is such as from necessity in some cases is substituted for stronger and better proof.

Secondment

Employment outside the Regular Army including ancilliary Corps or Service, *e.g.*, Defence Security Corps, National Cadet

Corps and Territorial Army when not embodied. *See* RA(DSR) – explanation of terms used.

Secrecy

The fact of making sure that nothing is known about something, the state of being secret. *See* Note to Army Act, section 52.

Securities

Property deposited or made over or bond, documents proving that somebody is the owner of shares; etc.in a particular company. *See* RA(DSR), para 821(a) and 826.

Security

All measures taken to safeguard information, personnel equipment and installations against undesirable activities of nations or individuals acting against the interest of the nation. Also means property deposited or made over by or on behalf of a person in order to secure his fulfilment of an obligation and forfeitable in the event of non-fulfilment. *See* Army Act, section 149.

Security of State

The expression includes serious and aggravated forms of public disorder but not all public disorder disrupts the security of the State. See *Romesh Thapar*, AIR 1950 SC 124.

Sedition

It requires a concert of action in resistance to a civil authority in the form of revolt, violence or disturbance against lawful civil authority. This offence consists in doing any act or publishing any words tending to bring into hatred or contempt, or to excite disaffection against the sovereign, or the Government. It is also seditious to incite subjects to attempt to procure otherwise then by lawful means the alteration of law, or to incite any person to commit any crime in disturbances of the peace or to raise discontent and disaffection among citizens, or to promote feelings of ill-will and hostility between different classes of citizens.

Seditious

Pertaining to or exciting sedition. *See* RA(DSR), para 1385(a)(ii).

Seduce

To persuade somebody to do something that they would not usually agree to do by making it seem very attractive. *See* Army Act, section 37(e).

Seizure

The provisional detention of ships or cargo by a belligerent, subject to confirmation by a prize court.

Seizure of Property

Seizure applies primarily to state property which is war booty. There are, however, certain cases mentioned in Article 53 of paragraph 2 of the Hague Convention in which private property can also be seized, but such seizure is only sequestration, to be followed by restitution and indemnity, whereas requisition implies a transfer of ownership. Requisition only affects private property. Articles susceptible of a direct military use are seized, articles not susceptible of a direct military use but useful for the needs of the occupying or advancing army are requisitioned.

Self Contained Code

A statute which does not need or depend upon any other Act and is able to operate and exist without help or influence of other laws.

Self-Deactivating

Automatically rendering a munition inoperable by means of the irreversible exhaustion of a component for example, a battery, that is essential to the operation of the munition. *See* Article 2.12 of the Protocol on Prohibitions or Restrictions on the Use of Mines, Booby-Traps and Other Devices, as amended on 3 May, 1996.

Self-Defence

A commander's inherent authority and obligation to use all necessary means available and to take all appropriate action in self-defence of the commander's unit and other forces in the vicinity. Action indispensable to forestall an imminent threat to a right or to redress the actual violation of such a right.

Self-Destruction Mechanism

An incorporated or externally attached automatically–functioning mechanism which secures the destruction of the munition into which it is incorporated or to which it is attached. *See* Article 2.10 of the Protocol on Prohibitions or Restrictions on the Use of Mines, Booby-Traps and Other Device, as amended on 3 May, 1996.

Self-Neutralization Mechanism

An incorporated automatically–functioning mechanism which renders inoperable the munition into which it is incorporated. *See* Article 2.11 of the Protocol on Prohibitions or Restrictions on the Use of Mines, Booby-Traps and Other Devices, as amended on 3 May, 1996.

Selling Price

Price in respect of dwelling unit/plot which the allottee has to pay to the Organisation prior to possession. *See* AWHO Master Brochure, July 1987.

Sentence

Decision, determination, final Judgment. A sentence may consist of one or more punishments.

Sentry

A soldier posted for protecting some place, property or person. *See* Note 5 to Army Act, section 36. A soldier may be placed in such a position as to be able to watch the approach of the enemy, to prevent surprises, to stop any person who would endeavour to pass his post without an order or without stating who he is.

Separation of Categories

Different categories of prisoners are to be kept in separate institutions or part of institutions taking account of their sex, age, criminal record, the legal reason for their detention and the necessities of their treatment.

Sepoy

Corrupted form of the Indian word *Sipahi*, "a soldier".

Sequestration

To take control of somebody's property or assets until a debt has been paid. The word finds mention in Army Act, section 62(e) pertaining to offences in relation to aircraft and flying.

Serious Crime

Conduct constituting an offence punishable by a maximum deprivation of liberty of at least four years or a more serious penalty. *See* Article 2(b) of the United Nations Convention Against Transnational Organised Crime.

Serious Injury or Damage

Means:

(i) serious bodily injury; or

(ii) extensive destruction of a place of public use, state or government facility, infrastructure facility, or public transport system, resulting in major economic loss; or

(iii) substantial damage to the environment, including air, soil, water, fauna or flora.

Serious Misconduct

Misconduct of so serious nature as to justify summary dismissal from service of a staff member found culpable by the Secretary General of such misconduct. [UN Secretary General Bulletin, 2003.]

The term also refers to any act, omission or negligence including criminal acts, that is a violation of mission standard operating procedures, directives, or any other applicable rules, regulations or administrative instructions that resulted in or is likely to result in serious damage or injury to an individual or to the mission.

DPKO-directive for Disciplinary Matters Involving Members of National Contingent (DPKO/MD/03/0099 3) gives following examples of "serious misconduct":—

* Sexual abuse and exploitation of any individual, particularly children.
* Harassment, including sexual harassment.
* Abuse of authority.
* Breach of confidentiality.
* Abuse of United Nations privileges and immunities.
* Use, possession or distribution of illegal narcotics.
* Embezzlement or other financial malfeasance.
* Wilful disobedience of a lawful order.

* Conduct prejudicial to good order and discipline
* Driving while intoxicated or other grossly negligent driving.
* Intoxicated while on duty in public on repeated occasions.
* Repeatedly absent from duty without permission
* Unlawful acts (*e.g.*, theft, fraud, smuggling, bribery) on or off United Nations premises with or without the involvement of United Nations vehicles, and whether or not the individual was officially on duty at the time of the offence.

Service

In a military sense is the art of serving the state in war. In a more restricted sense, service is the performance of military duty. In its general sense, service embraces all details of the military art.

Service Privileges

Are the benefits enjoyed by service personnel in their relation to civil courts and the law administered by these courts. These are conferred upon by the acts of Parliament and are mentioned in Chapter V of the Army Act.

Services Capital Acquisition Plan

It indicates the list of equipment to be acquired, keeping in view operational exigencies and the overall requirement of funds.

Services Qualitative Requirements

These express the user's requirements in terms of functional characteristics and are laid down in a comprehensive, structured and concrete manner by being broad-based and realistic.

Serving

The word 'serving' must be construed in wider sense in which a person employed by another is said to be serving merely by reason of relationship created by employment. [*Ajit Singh* v. *State of Punjab*, AIR 1970 P&H 351.]

Serving With

"Accompany" has been interpreted broader than "Serving with". *See* Army Act, section 2(1)(L).

Servitude

A limited right of an absolute character on somebody else's property. Existence in international law depends on consent, recognition or estoppel on other grounds.

Set Aside

To annul, quash or render void. The ordinary meaning of the word is to revoke or quash, the effect of which is to make the interim order inoperative or non-existent. See *Bileshwar Khan Udyog Khedli Sahkari Mandal Ltd.* v. *UOI*, AIR 1999 SC 1198. Under the UCMJ, an action by proper authority voiding the proceedings and the punishment awarded and restoring all rights, privileges, and property lost by virtue of the punishment imposed.

Set off

Where the period of imprisonment which can be shown in counter balance to liquidate the pre-trial or during trial period of custody.

Severance of Charges

The situation where an accused charged on a charge-sheet containing a number of charges and considering that he will be prejudiced in his defence if they are all tried at the same time applies in writing to the convening officer, or to the court, that he be tried separately on any charge on the charge-sheet.

Severe

Rigorous; strict or stern in dealings. *See* Army Act, sections 139(7) and 178.

Severe Reprimand

One of the punishments provided for, under the military law, that can be awarded by a court-martial or by way of a summary trial to a person of non-commissioned officer or higher rank.

Sexual Abuse

Actual or threatened physical intrusion of a sexual nature, whether by force or under unequal or coercive conditions.

[Section 1 of UN Secretary General's Bulletin, 2003.]

Sexual Behaviour

Includes any sexual behaviour not encompassed by the alleged offence. [US MRE 413(c)(1)(d).]

Sexually Explicit

The material in which the dominant theme depicts or describes nudity, including sexual or excretory activities or organs, in a lascivious way. [Military Honour and Decency Act, USA.]

Sexual Exploitation

An actual attempted abuse of positive vulnerability, differential power, or trust, for sexual purposes, including but not limited to profiting monetarily, socially or politically from the sexual exploitation of another.

[Section 1 of UN Secretary General's Bulletin, 2003.]

Sexual Predisposition

An alleged victim's mode of dress, speech or life style that does not directly refer to sexual activities or thoughts but that may have a sexual connotation for the fact-finder. [US MRE 412 (c)(1)(d).]

Sexual Slavery

Should be understood to be the status or condition of a person over whom any or all of the powers attaching to the right of ownership are exercised, including sexual access through rape or other forms of sexual violence.

[1926 Slavery Convention.]

Sexual Violence

Any act of gender based violence that results in, or is likely to result in physical, sexual or psychological harm or suffering to women, including threats of such acts, coercion or arbitrary deprivation of liberty, whether occurring in public or private life. *See* Article 1 of the Declaration on the Elimination of Violence Against women.

Shamefully

Shameful means a positive and disgraceful dereliction of duty and not merely negligence or misapprehension or error of Judgment. "Shamefully abandons or delivers" is an ingredient of a charge under Army Act, section 34.

Shifting of the Burden

When the prosecution have proved a *prima facie* case, it is not infrequently said that the burden of proof "shifts" on to the accused.

Ship

Except in the expression "on board a ship" includes an establishment of the Indian Navy commissioned as a ship in accordance with the custom of the Navy. *See* Navy Act, section 3(21). Also means a vessel of any type whatsoever not permanently attached to the sea bed, including dynamically supported crafts, submersibles, or any other floating craft.

Shipwrecked

Persons, whether military or civilian, who are in peril at sea or in other waters as a result of misfortune affecting them or the vessel or aircraft carrying them and who refrain from any act of hostility. These persons, provided that they continue to refrain from any act of hostility, shall continue to be considered shipwrecked during their rescue until they acquire another status under the Conventions or this Protocol.

Article 8(b) – Protocol Additional to the Geneva Conventions of 12 August 1949, and Relating to the Protection of Victims of International Armed Conflicts (Protocol I), 8 June 1977.

Shorthand Writer

An impartial person may at any time of the trial, if the count thinks it desirable, be sworn or affirmed to act as short-hand writer. *See* Army Rule 90(2).

Show Cause Notice

A notice or opportunity provided to make clear or apparent, as by evidence, testimony, or reasoning to prove. Where a superior or competent authority would allow the other side to answer. It is a chance given for leading evidence in support of the contentions raised against.

Signature

Your name as you usually write it, for example at the end of a letter. *See* Army Act, section 140.

Simultaneous Responsibility

Since a State only acts through its organs and officials, the same act can give rise both to responsibility of the State and the criminal liability of the individual. For example, if a military commander orders a direct attack on a civilian building, then this action may give rise to individual liability on the part of the commander and also the responsibility of the State to whose military forces he belongs, as his act is attributable to the State.

Sine Die

Without day or without assigning a day for further meeting or hearing, postponement without a date.

Sitting

The holding of a court. *See* Army Act, section 191(2)(f).

Small Arms

Are portable fire arms known as muskets, rifles, carbines, pistols, revolvers etc.

Small War

A vague name for any one of a great variety of military operations. As applied to the USA, small wars are operations undertaken under executive authority wherein military force is combined with diplomatic pressure in the internal or external affairs of another State whose Government is unstable, inadequate or unsatisfactory for the preservation of life and of such interests as are determined by the foreign policy. *See* US Marine Corps, Small Wars Manual.

Society

A group of people who join together for a particular purpose. *See* Army Act, section 21.

Sodomy

The offence of sodomy is committed when a male has carnal knowledge of an animal or of a human being *"per anum"*. Penetration is required, as in the case of rape, to constitute carnal knowledge.

Soldier

Any person who is a soldier or a sailor or an airman subject to the Army Act, 1950, the Navy Act, 1957, or the Air Force Act, 1950, as the case may be, and who is not a military officer. The expression practically includes all persons subject to military law other than officers. The term includes civilians subject to military law as such.

Sole Source Acquisition

A contract for the purchase of supplies or services that is entered into or proposed to be entered into by an agency after soliciting and negotiating with only one source.

Solicitation

The formal document used in negotiating acquisitions to communicate Government requirements to prospective contractors and to solicit proposals.

Solidarity

An explicit choice to side with a group of people and their political cause.

Sovereignty

Legal independence.

Specification

It is a plain, concise and definite statement of the essential facts constituting the offence charged. A specification is sufficient if it alleges every element of the charged offence expressly or by necessary implication. No particular format is required. *Ref.* UCMJ Rules for Court-Martial 307(c)(3).

Speaking Order

An order which contains matter which is explanatory or illustrative of the mere direction which is given by it.

Special Finding

Where the court finds that the facts proved in evidence differ materially from the facts alleged in the particulars of a charge, but are nevertheless sufficient to prove the offence charged and the difference is not so material as to have prejudiced the accused in his defence, it may record a special finding as to the particulars. *See* Army Rule 62(4) and (5).

Special Plea to Jurisdiction

An objection made by an accused on a plea that the court is improperly constituted, or that the accused is not subject to the Army Act, or that he is not liable to be tried by that description of court. *See* Army Rule 51(1) and Note 1 thereto.

Specified

Made clear. *See* Army Act, sections 81, 82 and 88(b).

Sponsorship

Relationship in which a company gives financial support to a component of the movement for a specific event, programme or project and in return expects public association of image. These are considered to be short-term, event-specific relationship. *See* Annex to Resolution 10 on Substantive Provisions of the International Red Cross and Red Crescent Movement Policy for Corporate Sector Partnerships.

Spy

A useful but not highly honoured auxiliary employed to ascertain the state of an enemy's affairs, and of his intended operations. They may be divided into two classes, firstly, those, who betray their own country to an enemy; secondly, those, who, being enemies, contrive surreptitiously to obtain information by penetrating into the opposing Army. According to the Hague Rules, a person can only be considered as a spy when, acting clandestinely or on false pretences, he obtains or endeavours to obtain information in the zone of operations of a belligerent with the intention of communicating it to the hostile party.

Squadron

Denotes two troops of cavalry. Three or four squadrons constitute a regiment. It is the unit by which the force of cavalry with an army is always computed.

Staff

The staff of an Army consists of a body of skilled officers whose duty it is to combine and give vitality to the movement and mechanical action of the several regiments and drilled bodies composing the force. The staff may include general staff, the personal staff, Adjutant General, Quarter Master General, Master General of Ordnance, the civil or departmental staff, recruiting staff, pensioner staff, regimental staff, the garrison staff etc.

Staff Judge Advocate

A judge advocate so designated in Army, Air Force, or Marine Corps, and means the principal legal adviser of a command in the Navy and Coast Guard who is a judge advocate. *See* RCM US 103(17).

Standing Order

These are certain general rules and instructions, which are to be invariably followed, and are not subject to the temporary intervention of rank. These are not to be altered by temporary commander.

State

The State as a person (*i.e.*, subject) of international law should possess the following qualifications,

(a) a permanent population;
(b) a defined territory;
(c) a Government; and
(d) capacity to enter into relations with other States.

State of War

A special social status of the country, which is declared in the period from the time the country is invaded to the time such act of invasion is de facto terminated. Article 3.5 of the Vietnam's Law of National Defence.

State Responsibility

A delictual or civil liability of the State arising from a failure to fulfil its international obligations—gives rise to an obligation to make reparation.

Stateless Person

An individual who is not a national of any State.

Station

A general term meaning any army, naval or air activity at a fixed land location; a particular kind of activity to which other activities or individuals may come for a specific service often of a technical nature. Each station will be classified by the service in which it operates permanently or temporarily.

Station Commander (*See* Officer Commanding the Station).

Status

The legal position of an individual in or with regard to the rest of the community. The rights, duties, capacities, incapacities which determine a person to a given class constitute his status. *See* Army Act, section 142(2).

Status of Forces Agreement

Subjection to foreign jurisdiction may be provided by treaties or other international agreements between the sending State and the host or receiving State. Such an agreement is called a Status of Forces Agreement (SOFA). A SOFA is a pact between nations specifying which nation has jurisdiction in particular situations. SOFAs are not purely jurisdictional; they also provide some guarantees to accused persons.

Stipulated

Arranged or settled definitely, as agreement or covenant, stated clearly and firmly that something must be done, or how it must be done. *See* Army Rule 16A.

Stoppages

It is an amount meant only to compensate for loss or damage caused by an offender. It can be awarded by a court-martial or summarily or administratively. *See* Army Act, sections 71(l), 80, 83, 84, 85, 90(g) and 91(g). These can be awarded to make good any loss, expenses or damage occasioned by the accused's offence, and must not exceed the amount necessary to do this.

Strategic Alliance

Relationships formed between a company and a component of the movement that are focussed on jointly addressing a goal of common interest (*e.g.*, resolving a specific social problem) and involve the public association of image. These relationships are often multifaceted, long-term, and pool the complementary strengths of two organizations. *See* Annex to Resolution 10 on Substantive Provisions of the International Red Cross and Red Crescent Movement Policy for Corporate Sector Partnerships.

Stress

In individuals is defined as any interference that disturbs a person's healthy mental and physical well-being. It occurs when the body is required to perform beyond its normal range of capabilities.

Strikes

An intentional blow, and includes any offensive touching of a person, however slight.

Study Leave

It is a type of extra-ordinary leave for the grant of which all regular officers are eligible for pursuing special studies in India or Ex-India. [Army Order 11/1987.]

Sub-Area

Any of the Sub-Areas into which India is for military purposes for the time being divided, and includes, for all or any of the purposes of this Act, any territory which the Central Government may by notification in the Official Gazette, declare to be a sub-area for such purposes. *See* section 2 (xxx vii-a) of the Cantonment Act, 1924.

Subaltern

A commissioned officer below the rank of captain.

Sub-contracting

Refers to a class of organisations that make their living by executing contracts for donor Governments and, to a lesser extent, multilateral institutions.

Subdue

To bring under, to conquer by force or the exertion of superior power.

Subjects of International Law

Entities with international personality.

Subjugate

To subdue and bring under the yoke of power or dominion.

Sub-let

To rent to somebody else all or part of a property that you rent from the owner. *See* RA(DSR), para 1016.

Subordinate Officer

A person appointed as an acting sub Lieutenant, a midshipman or a cadet in any branch of the Indian Navy or the Indian Naval Reserve Forces, but does not include a cadet whilst under training in a joint service institute. *See* section 3(23) of the Navy Act, 1957.

Subsist

To support with provisions; to feed, to maintain.

Subsistence Allowance

A fraction of total monetary entitlement paid to one under custody so as to enable him to provide for the want of his family members.

Substance

That which is essential, essence.

Sub Unit

Part of a unit, *e.g.*, company, battery or squadron etc. In a military sense, means a small body of foot or artillery, the number of which is never fixed, but in generally from 50 to 120.

Substitution

Adding by way of amendment to remove an existing anomaly. *See* Army Act, section 163(4).

Subversion

It is an act calculated to undermine or divert the loyalty of any person with a view to rendering him ineffective in the organisation he belongs to or make cooperate with unfriendly or enemy country or a dissident or disaffected group.

Subversive of Discipline

The accused's conduct must have been not only to the prejudice of discipline but actually calculated to destroy it.

Succession

The regular pattern of one thing following another, a number of people or things that follow each other in time or order. *See* Army Rule 87(2).

Successive Trial

A person convicted or acquitted by a court-martial may, after obtaining requisite sanction, be tried again by a criminal court for the same offence, or on the same facts. [Army Rule 127.]

Sue

To institute a suit. *See* RA(DSR), para 534.

Sufficient

Enough for a particular purpose, as much as you need. *See* Army Act, section 39.

Sum Certain Requirement

Failure to specify a sum certain will result in denial of the claim and will preclude a subsequent federal tort claim action. The amount of damages stated in the claim constitutes the upper limit of the award.

Summarily

Generally implies a trial without a jury and without adopting the elaborate formalities prescribed for ordinary trials.

Summary Award

Officers below the rank of Lieutenant Colonel, JCOs and WOs may be summarily dealt with by one of the superior authorities specified in Army Act, sections 83 and 84. Also *see* RA(DSR), para 444.

Summary Court-Martial

One of the types of court-martial held by the commanding officer of the corps, department or detachment. It can try all persons subject to the Army Act and under command of the officer holding the trial other than officers, JCOs and WOs. *See* Army Act, section 120(3).

Summary Disposal

Trial of an officer, a junior commissioned officer or a warrant officer in the manner indicated in Army Rule 26 without invoking a court-martial for relatively less grave offences.

Summary of Evidence

It is a record of un-sworn statements bearing on the charges against an accused taken under orders of his commanding officer and includes statement of accused (if any) made by him voluntarily and of witnesses, if any, called by him in defence. *See* Army Rule 23.

Summary Procedure

Simplified and abridged judicial procedure.

Summary Punishment

These are the punishments that can be inflicted by a commanding officer without recourse to a court-martial. *See* Army Act, sections 80, 81 and 85.

Summary Reduction

Army Act, sections 20(2), (4) and (6) provide for the summary reduction of WOs and NCOs. Such administrative reduction may be ordered if the WO or NCO is found inefficient or unfit to hold the position in which he was placed.

Summary Trial

A form of trial in which the established formal course of a legal proceeding is disregarded. It means immediate, instantaneous process without delays.

Summing up

When the closing addresses have been given at a court-martial, the Judge Advocate will sum up the evidence and advise the court upon the law relating to the case. *See* Army Rules 60, 68 and 105(5).

Summon

To order somebody to appear in court. *See* RA(DSR), para 531.

Summoning of Witnesses

The process of securing attendance of a witness for the court of inquiry, summary of evidence or the trial.

Superannuated

Incapacitated for service, either from age or infirmity, and placed on a pension.

Superior Officer

When used in relation to a person subject to the Army Act includes a junior commissioned officer, warrant officer and a non-commissioned officer, and as regards persons placed under his orders, an officer, warrant officer, petty officer and non-commissioned officer of the Navy or Air Force. *See* section 3(xxiii) of the Army Act. Also relates to any officer of higher rank, or who has priority in the same rank, by the date of his commission etc.

Supernumerary Members

They are detailed for a court-martial. They are sworn and sit and are present at all deliberations even when the court is cleared, in order to be prepared to take the place of any absent member. Until then they have no voice.

Supersede

It is to deprive an officer of rank and pay for any offence or neglect or to place one officer over the head of another, who may or may not be more deserving.

Suppress

To put an end, often by force, to a group or an activity that is believed to threaten authority. *See* Army Act, section 37(c).

Surrender

To lay down your arm, and give yourself up as a prisoner of war. Also the act of giving up, as the surrender of a town or garrison. *See* Army Act, section 142(6).

Surprise

Is an action or series of actions, which are sudden in occurrence, forceful in thrust and completely unanticipated to achieve a decisive outcome.

Survivability

The degree to which a system is able to avoid or withstand a man-made hostile environment without suffering an abortive impairment of its ability to accomplish its designated mission.

Suspect

Is a person concerning whom the Prosecutor possesses reliable information, which tends to show that he may have committed a crime, one over which the tribunal has jurisdiction. *See* Article 2 of the Rules of Procedure and Evidence of the ICTY.

Suspend

The act of temporarily depriving an officer of rank and pay, in consequence of some offence. To delay, to protract, hence, to suspend hostilities.

Suspension

Action by proper authority to withhold the execution of a punishment for a probationary period.

Suspension from Service

An officer may be suspended from duty (independent of arrest) by his officer commanding or any other superior authority, not only when he himself submits his case for investigation, but also in any case in which his character or conduct as an officer and a gentleman is impugned. While under suspension, an officer will be placed under the same restrictions as an officer in open arrest. *See* RA(DSR), para 349.

Suspension of Arms

It is essentially a military convention of very short duration, concluded between commanders of armies or detachments in order to arrange some pressing local interest; most frequently to bury the dead or to collect and succour the wounded, or sometimes to exchange prisoners, or to permit conferences, or to enable a commander to communicate with his Government or a superior in order to request or obtain orders.

Suspension of Sentence

This applies only to a sentence of imprisonment for life or imprisonment. The convict is released from custody though sentence continues to run. *See* Army Act, sections 182 to 185.

Sustainability

The ability to maintain the necessary level and duration of combat activity to achieve national objectives. Sustainability is a function of providing and maintaining those levels of force material and consumables necessary to support a military effort.

Suzerain

Lord paramount, especially in relation to internally autonomous or semi-independent vassal States.

Symbol

Is an object, art, event, quality or relationship that serves as a vehicle for conveying meaning and giving a physical shape to the whole perspective.

T

Technology

Any information (including information embodied in software) other than information in the public domain, that is capable of being used in—

(a) the development, production or use of any goods or software;

(b) the development of, or the carrying out of, an industrial or commercial activity or the provisions of a service of any kind.

Explanation—When technology is described wholly or partly by reference to the user to which it (or the goods to which it relates) may be put, it shall include services which are provided or used, or which are capable of being used, in the development, production or use of such technology or goods. *See* section 4(l) of the Weapons of Mass Destruction and their Delivery Systems (Prohibition of Unlawful Activities) Act, 2005.

Temporary Duty

Any move on duty which as per the expectation of the ordering authority is that the individual shall do duty in the station to which his move is ordered for a period of 180 days or less. [Travel Regulations, para 91.]

Terminal Leave

Leave granted as a welfare measure to a short service commissioned officer on expiry of his contract period. *See* Army Instruction 28/S/1948.

Termination

Termination is inter-changeable with the word 'removal'. It signifies removal or dismissal as penalty or punishment for misconduct. *See* Army Rule 14.

Territorial Army

A military force of people who are not professional soldiers but who train as soldiers in their free time. Voluntary military force organised on a territorial basis, it was founded in 1908 and known as Territorial Force. They are second line army. They play a very vital role in the war and natural calamities. *See* Introduction to TA Act, 1948.

Territorial Jurisdiction

The competence of a State within its territory.

Territorial Principle

This principle of criminal jurisdiction determines jurisdiction by reference to the place where the offence was committed, or where its constituent effects took place. In the context of fight against international terrorism, implies that every nation has the authority to establish and enforce criminal laws regarding conduct within its own territory.

Territorial Sea

A belt of sea adjacent to the coast of a State and situated between its internal waters and the high seas over which the coastal State exercises a limited territorial jurisdiction.

Territoriality of Criminal Law

The doctrine that municipal criminal law is concerned only with offences committed within the territorial jurisdiction of a State.

Territory

A specific portion of the surface of the globe, together with its subsoil and superjacent air space, under the jurisdiction of a subject of international law. The word 'territory' in relation to "*Levee en Masse*" is not intended to mean the whole extent of a belligerent State, but refers to any part of it which is not yet invaded.

Terrorism

Calculated use of violence or threat of violence to inculcate fear, intended to coerce or to intimidate Governments or societies in the pursuit of goals that are generally political, religious or ideological. [US Army, Operational Law Handbook, 2005 Edn., Page 380.] Premeditated, politically motivated violence perpetrated against non-combatant targets by sub-national groups or clandestine agents, usually intended to influence an audience. Activities that involve violent acts or acts dangerous to human life that are a violation of the criminal laws and appear to be intended to intimidate or coerce a civilian population, to influence the policy of a Government by intimidation or coercion, or to affect the conduct of a Government by mass destruction, assassination or kidnapping.

Terrorism Investigation

Is a fact finding procedure to search out, develop, assemble and record all available information regarding suspected terrorist activities.

Terrorist

A person who indulges in wanton killing of persons or involves in violence or in the disruption of services or means of communications essential to the community or in damaging property with a view to putting the public or any section of the public in fear; or affecting adversely the harmony between different religious, racial, language groups or overawing the sovereignty and integrity of a nation. *Vide* section 2(1)(y), it means any person who, with intent to overawe the Government as by law established or to strike terror in the people or any section of the people or to alienate any section of the people or to adversely affect the harmony amongst different sections of the people, does any act or thing by using bombs, dynamite or other explosive substances or inflammable substances or firearms or other lethal weapons or poisons or noxious gases or other chemicals or any other substances (whether biological or otherwise) of a hazardous nature, in such a manner as to cause, or is likely to cause, death of, or injuries to, any person or persons or damage to, or destruction of, property or disruption of any supplies or services essential to the life of the community.

Terrorist Acts

Are peacetime equivalents of war crimes.

Terrorist Gang

Any association, other than terrorist organisation, whether systematic or otherwise, which is concerned with, or involved in, terrorist act. *See* section 2(1)(l) of the Unlawful Activities (Prevention) Act, 1967.

The Forces

The regular Army, Navy and Air Force or any part of any one or more of them. *See* Army Act, section 3(xi).

Theft or Larceny

A person steals who, without the consent of the owner, fraudulently, and without a claim of right made in good faith, "takes" and "carries away" anything "capable of being stolen" with intent, at the time of such taking, permanently to deprive the owner thereof.

Threat

It is an expressed present determination or intent to kill, injure, or intimidate a person or to damage or destroy certain property presently or in the future.

Threaten

To intimidate by threats; seem to impend evil, threaten person with penalty or prosecution or punishment.

Threatening language

Language from which a person addressed may reasonably infer that criminal force may be used. This may be inferred from the character of the words used or from the surrounding circumstances. *See* Notes 12 and 13 to Army Act, section 40.

Tort feasor

A person who commits a tort.

Torture

The intentional infliction of severe pain or suffering, whether physical or mental, upon a person in the custody or under the control of the accused; except that torture shall not include pain or suffering only from, inherent in or incidental to, lawful sanctions. *See* Article 2.1(e) of the ICC Statute. According to the Torture Convention, the pain or suffering must be inflicted on a person for such purposes as obtaining information or a confession, punishing or intimidating or coercing or for any reason based on discrimination of any kind. Further, the pain or suffering must be inflicted by or at the instigation of or with the consent or acquiescence of a public official or other person acting in an official capacity. According to 1985 Inter-American Convention to Prevent and Punish Torture, the term shall be understood to be any act intentionally performed whereby physical or mental pain or suffering is inflicted on a person for purposes of criminal investigation, as a means of intimidation, as personal punishment, as a preventive measure, as a penalty or for any other purposes. Torture shall also be understood to be the use of methods upon a person intended to obliterate the personality of the victim or to diminish his physical or mental capacities, even if they do not cause physical pain or mental anguish. The crime can be committed by act and omission.

Total War

A nation is involved in a total war when the complete resources available to it contribute towards the war effort. A war may be total for the belligerents and limited for the non-belligerents.

Tracing

In the context of fire-arms, means the systematic tracking of fire-arms and where possible, their parts and components and ammunition from manufacture to purchase for the purpose of assisting the competent authorities of State Parties in detecting, investigating and analysing illicit manufacturing and illicit trafficking. [Article 3(f) of the Protocol against the Illicit Manufacturing of and Trafficking in Fire-arms, their Parts and Components and Ammunition, Supplementing the United Nations Convention against Transnational Organised Crime.]

Trading with Enemy

Dealings between persons resident in the territory of belligerent with persons resident in enemy or enemy controlled territory.

Trailer

A carriage constructed or adapted for being drawn by a mechanically propelled carriage.

Training Year

For the purpose of the Territorial Army Act Rules, 1948, means a period of twelve months beginning on the first day of April and ending on the thirty first day of March.

Traitor

One who violates his allegiance and betrays his country; one guilty of treasons; one who, in breach of trust, delivers his country to its enemy, or any fort or place entrusted to its defence; or who surrenders an army or body of troops to the enemy, unless when vanquished, or one who takes arms and levies war against his country; or one who aides an enemy in conquering his country.

Transcript

Copy of any original writing or deed etc.; anything written from an original. *See* Army Rule 46.

Transfer

Transfer is the term applied when a soldier is moved from the Corps in which he is serving to another Corps, or to the Reserve. A soldier can be transferred at any time with his own consent. He can only be transferred to another Corps without his consent so far as the Military Law allows. The term also involves, in addition to the physical movement of mines into or from national territory, the transfer of title to and control over the mines, but does not involve the transfer of territory containing emplaced mines. *See* Article 2.15 of the Protocol on Prohibitions or Restrictions on the Use of Mines, Booby-Traps and Other Devices as Amended on 3 May, 1996.

Transit State

A State, other than the host State, in whose territory United Nations and associated personnel or their equipment are in transit or temporarily present in connection with a United Nations operation.

Transmission

Conveyance from one person or place to another, the action of transmitting or the fact of being transmitted.

Transportation

The banishing or sending away a criminal into another country. Transportation is by way of punishment of one convicted of offence against the laws of the country.

Trans-shipment

To remove goods from the conveyance on which they were brought into India and to place the goods on the same or another conveyance for the purpose of taking them out of India, where these acts are carried out on a "through bill of lading", "through airway bill" or "through manifest".

Explanation—"Through bill of lading", "through airway bill" and "through manifest" mean respectively a bill of lading, airway bill and manifest, for the consignment of goods from a place outside India to a destination which is also outside India without a consignee in India.

See section 4(n) of the Weapons of Mass Destruction and their Delivery Systems (Prohibition of Unlawful Activity) Act, 2005.

Travelling Allowance

Is an allowance made to officers and soldiers when travelling under proper orders.

Treacherously

Treacherously implies an intention to assist the enemy and must be carefully distinguished from 'through cowardice'. *See* Note 9 to Army Act, section 34.

Treason

A general appellation to denote not only offences against the State but also that accumulation of guilt which arises whenever a superior reposes confidence in a subject or inferior, between whom and himself there exists a natural, a civil, or even a spiritual relation, and the inferior so abuses that confidence, so forgets the obligations of duty, subjection, and allegiance, as to destroy the life of any such superior or lord. It also includes imagining the Sovereign's death or that of the heir to the throne, levying war against the Sovereign in any of his Dominions, aiding the enemies of the Sovereign etc.

Treason Felony

These offences include an intention to deprive the King of his crown or Royal dignity; to levy war on him to force him to change his measures, or to put constraint on either House of Parliament; or to stir up foreigners to invade the Realm or the King's Dominions.

Treatise

A long and serious piece of writing on a particular subject.

Treaty

The Vienna convention on the Law of Treaties, 1969, defines in its Article 2.1 to mean an international agreement concluded between States in written form and governed by international law, whether embodied in a single instrument or in two or more related instruments and whatever its particular designation. The treaty process includes negotiations, signing, ratification, exchange of ratifications, publishing and proclamation and treaty execution.

Tri Service

In relation to the quantum of force or approach or resources etc. means the Army, Navy and the Air Force.

Trial Counsel

Under the UCMJ, the judge advocate who serves as the prosecutor in courts-martial.

U

Ultimatum

Final statement of terms, rejection of which may lead to the rupture of diplomatic relations or war.

Ultra Vires

Beyond a person's power and jurisdiction.

Unauthorised Punishment

A punishment that is in any respect at variance with the Army Act, Army Rules or the Regulations. *See* RA(DSR), para 353.

Unbecoming

Not suiting a particular person, not appropriate or acceptable. *See* Army Act, section 45.

Unbecoming Conduct

Conduct not befitting the position of an officer, JCO or WO as the case may be. It may be of a military or social character. The conduct should be viewed having regard to its nature and the circumstances in which it took place. *See* Notes to Army Act, section 45.

Unexploded Ordnance

Explosive ordnance that has been primed, fused, armed or otherwise prepared for use and used in an armed conflict. It may have been fired, dropped, launched or projected and should have exploded but failed to do so.

See Article 2.2 of the Protocol on Explosive Remnants of War (Protocol V to the 1980 Convention).

Under Command

Is being liable to be ordered on any particular duty.

Underground

An unarmed person who generally operates clandestinely belonging to a group/body of people whose activities are concerned with resistance to lawfully constituted Government and the security forces. Such groups/body of people has been declared an unlawful organization by an Act of Parliament. Generally belonging to executive/civil set up of the unlawful organisation.

Undertaking

A promise, stipulation or engagement to do something. *See* Army Rule 147A.

Unfair

Not fair, marked by injustice, partiality or deception.

Unfitness

The term should be construed broadly, including, for *e.g.*, matters relating to the incompetence, impartiality and misconduct of the judge.

Unfit to Stand Trial

Unable on account of mental disorder to conduct a defence at any stage of a trial by court-martial before a finding is made or to instruct counsel to do so, and in particular, unable on account of mental disorder to:

(a) understand the nature or object of the proceedings,

(b) understand the possible consequences of the proceedings, or

(c) communicate with counsel.

Section 2 of the Canada's National Defence Act, 1985.

Unified Command

A command with a broad continuing mission under a single commander and composed of significant assigned components of two or more services operates under an officer specifically assigned to the command thereof by the Joint Chiefs of Staff or the commander of a unified command.

Uniform

In its military sense, means the particulars dress and equipment assigned by proper authority to each grade of officers and men.

Uniform Code of Military Justice

The enactment by the US Congress when it undertook the process of unifying military law and procedure by creating a uniform code to govern the Army, Navy, Marine Corps, Air Force and Coast Guard. Referred to as the "UCMJ", it forms the basis for military criminal law. It contains the requirements for jurisdiction, trial procedure, sentencing, and non-judicial punishment.

Unilateral

One-sided.

Unilateral Act

Legally relevant or binding declaration on the part of a State of its intention to do or abstain from doing something.

Unit

Under Air Force Act, section 3(xxviii) the term includes:—z

(a) Any body of officers and airmen for which a separate authorised establishment exists.

(b) Any separate body of persons subject to the Air Force Act on any service and not attached to a unit as aforesaid.

(c) Any other separate body of persons composed wholly or partly or persons subject to the Air Force Act, and specified as a unit by the Central Government.

Unitary State

A State in which the supreme authority rests in one centre.

United Nations Operation

An operation established by the competent organ of the United Nations in accordance with the Charter of the United Nations and conducted under United Nations authority and control:

(i) Where the operation is for the purpose of maintaining or restoring international peace and security; or

(ii) Where the Security Council or the General Assembly has declared, for the purpose of this Convention, that there exists an exceptional risk to the safety of the personnel participating in the operation.

[1994 Convention on the Safety of the United Nations and Associated Personnel.]

United Nations Personnel

Means:

(i) Persons engaged or deployed by the Secretary General of the United Nations as members of the military, police or civilian components of a United Nations operation;

(ii) Other officials and experts on mission of the United Nations or its specialised agencies or the International Atomic Energy Agency who are present in the area where a United Nations operation is being conducted.

[1994 Convention on the Safety of the United Nations and Associated Personnel.]

Universal

Global scope, *e.g.*, of international law or of an institution.

Universality Principle

This principle of criminal jurisdiction determines jurisdiction by reference to the place of custody of the person committing the offence. In the context of fight against international terrorism implies that a nation has the authority to establish and enforce criminal laws regarding conduct universally dangerous to nations, wherever it occurs. Piracy has traditionally been considered to be such conduct. Genocide, crimes against humanity, slave trading and aircraft hijacking probably also qualify.

Unjust

Contrary to justice, not just characterised by injustice. The word has a connotation to Army Act, section 87 with regard to review of proceedings.

Unlawful

That which is contrary to law laid down in Statute or unauthorised by law. Under the Weapons of Mass Destruction and their Delivery Systems (Prohibition of Unlawful Activities) Act, 2005, section 4(o) it means, "without the authority of the Central Government and the expression 'unlawfully' shall be construed accordingly".

Unlawful Assembly

It is an assembly of five or more persons the common object of which is to—(a) overawe Government or any public servant in exercise of his legal power, (b) to resist execution of any legal process, (c) to commit mischief, criminal trespass or other offence, (d) forcibly to take possession of, or deprive any person of, property or incorporeal right, (e) forcibly to compel a person to do (or omit to do) any act. An assembly lawful, when it assembled may subsequently become unlawful. *See* IPC, sections 141, 142, 425 and 441.

Unlawful Combatants

A person who has forfeited the combatant privilege by not respecting the basic rules of distinction. *See* Article 44(3) of AP I.

Unlawful Confinement

Deprivation of liberty that is not in conformity with the various rules provided for in the Convention. *See* GC IV, Article 147.

Unlawful Entry

When made without the consent of any person authorised to consent to entry or without other lawful authority.

Unlawfully

The word has been used in Army Act, section 61 and at other places. Unlawful detaining means detaining contrary to law.

Unlimited Rights

Rights to use, duplicate, release, or disclose technical data or computer software in whole or in part in any manner and for any purpose, and to have or permit others to do so.

Unmanned Aerial Vehicle

An unmanned aircraft of any size which does not carry a weapon and which cannot control a weapon. *See* HPCR Draft Manual on Air and Missile Warfare.

Unmanned Combat Aerial Vehicle

An unmanned aircraft of any size which carries and delivers force, lethal or non-lethal, or which can use on-board technology to direct such force to a target. *See* HPCR Draft Manual on Air and Missile Warfare.

Unnatural Act

Whoever voluntarily has carnal intercourse against the order of nature with any man, woman or animal commits an unnatural offence. *See* IPC, section 377.

Unprivileged Belligerents

These may include spies, saboteurs, or civilians who are participating in the hostilities or who otherwise engage in unauthorised attacks or other combatant acts. They are not entitled to prisoner of war status, and may be prosecuted under the domestic law of the captor.

Unprotected Civilians

A sub-group of the civilians which does not enjoy civilian immunity. They take direct part in hostilities and may, therefore, be attacked. *See* Article 50, Para 1, AP I. They do not enjoy any combatant privilege and may be punished for participation in hostilities, subject to the procedural projection of Article 45, AP I.

Unreasonable

Opposite of reasonable; not agreeable to reason. *See* Army Act, section 137(1).

Unsuitable

Not right or appropriate for a particular person, purpose or occasion. *See* Army Rule 16A.

Untried Prisoners

Persons arrested or imprisoned by reason of a criminal charge against them, who are detained either in police custody or in prison custody but have not yet been tried and sentenced.

Unwed Parents

Army Regulation 601-210, Rule G of the US Army prohibits unmarried parents of children aged 18 years or younger from enlisting or remaining enlisted in the Army. This is a non-waivable restriction.

Urban Unit

A unit having training throughout the year on the weekly drill system and at an annual camp. *See* Rule 2(h) of the Territorial Army Rules, 1948.

Usage

The way in which words are used in a language, the fact of something being used; how much something is used. *See* Army Act, section 2(xiii).

Utmost

Taking those measures which may properly be called for by the circumstances, including the rank, responsibilities, or employment of the person concerned.

V

Vacate

To annul, to make void, to deprive of force, to vacate a commission, to make of no authority or validity.

Validity

The state of being legally or officially acceptable. *See* Army Act, section 193A.

Variation

This is properly expressing a sentence which is informally expressed; or, if a sentence be in excess of punishment authorised by law, varying it so that it shall not be in such excess. A thing that is different from other things in the same general group. *See* Army Rules 4 and 73.

Vehicle

A wheeled conveyance of any description which is capable of being used on a street, and includes a motor car, motor lorry, motor omnibus, cart, locomotive tram car, hand card, truck, motor cycle, bicycle, tricycle and rickshaw. *See* section 2(xxxviii) of the Cantonment Act, 1924.

Verdict

The answer of a jury given to the court, concerning the matter of fact in any cause committed to their trial; a finding, conclusion or judgment upon some matter or subject. *See* Army Rule 120.

Verification

Making out to be true, formal assertion of truth, the action of establishing or testing the truth.

Verify

To assent or approve to be true; to ascertain, confirm or test the truth or accuracy of. *See* RA(DSR), para 547.

Vessel

Includes every description of watercraft or other artificial contrivance used or capable of being used, as a means of transportation on water.

Victims of Abuse of Power

In Article 18 of the Victims Declaration, the term is defined as persons who, individually or collectively, have suffered harm, including physical or mental injury, emotional suffering, economic loss or substantial impairment of their fundamental rights, through acts or omissions that do not yet constitute violations of national criminal laws but of internationally recognised norms relating to human rights.

Victims of Crime

The Victims Declaration vide its Article 1 defines as 'victims of crime' persons who, individually or collectively, have suffered harm, including physical or mental injury, emotional suffering, economic loss or substantial impairment of their fundamental rights, through acts or omissions that are in violations of criminal laws operative within Member States, including those laws proscribing abuse of power.

Victualling Houses

This term includes inns or hotels (whether licensed or not), alehouses, livery stables, places where spirits, etc.are sold by retail. The liability to furnish billets lies on all keepers of these houses.

Views

Where a court considers it necessary to view any place or thing before the finding.

Visit and Search

The right of a belligerent man-of-war to stop a neutral merchant ship on the high seas or in enemy waters and search her on suspicion that the ship is carrying contraband or is engaged in unneutral services.

Visitor

One who visits officially for the purpose of inspection or supervision. *See* Army Act, sections 146(b) and 177(b).

Voluntarily

In the context of Army Act, section 34(j) means of his own free will *i.e.*, it means merely that the accused was willing to do the act charged.

Volunteer

Men who voluntarily come forward to serve in a force for the country. In general acceptance of the word, any one who enters the service on his own accord.

Voting

Every member of court-martial must give, by word of mouth, his opinion on any incidental question, finding and sentence. The opinions must be taken in succession beginning with the member lowest in rank. If the votes given are equal, the decision shall favour the accused. The Presiding Officer has no second or casting vote upon the finding and sentence. The majority of votes will decide the issue. It is to be noted that while mere seating of members not according to their seniority may be an irregularity, but, voting not beginning with member lowest in rank as per their seniority is an illegality, and the same cannot be cured subsequently.

Voucher

Document establishing payment of money or truth of accounts, a receipt which may serve as evidence of payment or discharge of debt. *See* Army Act, section 58(a).

W

Waiting Member

These are named in the convening order and are meant to fill place of those members who are not available to serve due to non-eligibility, disqualification, challenge or otherwise. Those not so required must withdraw before court is sworn or affirmed. *See* Army Rule 37(3) and Notes 5 thereto.

Wanton

It includes "reckless", but in describing the operation or physical control of a vehicle, vessel, or aircraft "wanton" may, in a proper case, connote wilfulness, or a disregard of probable consequences.

War

A legal condition of armed hostility between States usually accompanied by the commission of acts of violence. A state, in which subject to the operation of the rules of war and neutrality, States may apply against one another all forms of pressure.

War Correspondents

These are journalists who accompany the armed forces of a State without being members thereof. They are civilians and may not be made the object of attack. *See* Article 50(1) AP I. They are entitled to prisoner-of-war status upon capture. [Article 4(A)(4) GC III.]

War Crime

Grave breaches of the Geneva Conventions, 1949; other serious violations of the laws and customs applicable in international armed conflict within the established framework of international law and in the case of an armed conflict not of an international character, serious violations of Article 3 common to the four Geneva Conventions, 1949. *See* Article 8 of the ICC Statute. The term 'war crime' is the technical expression for such an act of enemy soldiers and enemy civilians as may be visited by punishment or capture of the offenders.

War, Time of

A period of war declared by congress or the factual determination by the President that the existence of hostilities warrants a finding that a time of war exists. *See* RCM US 103(11).

Warned

Admonished of some duty to be performed at a given time or place. Thus, officers and soldiers are warned for guard etc.

Warnings

The punctual provision of cautionary information to the civilian population, intended to minimise risks caused by explosive remnants of war in affected territories. *See* Technical Annex to the Protocol on Explosive Remnants of war.

Warning For Trial

The process, prior to the trial, when an accused is informed of every charge for which he is to be tried and asked to give the names of witnesses whom he desires to call in his defence. A copy and translation of the charge sheet is usually supplied to the accused. *See* Army Rule 34.

Warrant

The forms empowering the process of convening and confirming of General Court-Martial or District Court-Martial proceedings. These are classified as A-1, A-2, A-3 and B-1 warrants.

Warrant Officer

One of the ranks senior in status to the Non Commissioned Officer, means a person appointed gazetted or in pay as a warrant officer of the regular officer of the Indian Reserve Forces and includes a warrant officer of the Indian Supplementary Reserve Forces or of the Territorial Army who is, for the time being, subject to the Army Act. *See* Army Act, section 3(xxiii).

Watch-word

Is a parole differing from countersign in that it is only communicated to officers of guards, while the countersign is given to all the members. The watch-word is usually the name of a distinguished officer, while the countersign is the name of a place, as of a battlefield. Watch-word will include any authorised pass-word not being parole or countersign, which might for example, be adopted for a particular emergency.

Weapons of Mass Destruction

Any biological, chemical or nuclear weapons. *See* section 4(p) of the Weapons of Mass Destruction and their Delivery Systems (Prohibition of Unlawful Activities) Act, 2005.

Whipping

An act of hitting somebody with lashes. *See* Army Act, section 69.

Will

Kindred roll prepared by the military authorities about the disposal of a soldier's property on the information furnished by the soldier, held, is not a will. See *Ratnammal* v. *Thilalammal,* AIR 1957 AP 336.

Wilfully

In a wilful manner, purposely, intentionally or deliberately, especially intending the natural and probable consequences of the act.

Withdrawal

The term relates to an order to a cadet in a military academy to discontinue his training, on disciplinary, medical, training or other grounds.

Withhold

It connotes withdrawal or deprivation, *i.e.*, by his failing to do what he was bound to do and what was within his power and control to do. One of the options available to a superior authority in respect of court-martial proceedings is to withhold confirmation.

Witness

One who gives evidence before a judicial tribunal or who testifies in a cause.

With Intent to Defraud

An essential ingredient of a charge in respect of offences in respect of property. This has two necessary elements essential to the commission of the crime; namely first, deceit or an intention to deceive or in some cases mere secrecy, and secondly, either actual injury or possible injury or an intent to expose some person either to actual injury or to a risk of possible injury by means of that deceit or secrecy. *See* Note 24 to Army Act 52.

"Wounded" and "Sick"

Persons, whether military or civilian, who, because of trauma, disease or other physical or mental disorder or disability, are in need of medical assistance or care and who refrain from any act of hostility. These terms also cover maternity cases, new-born babies and other persons who may be in need of immediate medical assistance or care, such as the infirm or expectant mothers, and who refrain from any act of hostility.

[Article 8(a) – Protocol Additional to the Geneva Conventions of 12 August, 1949, and Relating to the Protection of Victims of International Armed Conflicts (Protocol I), 8 June, 1977.]

Wounded in Action

A battle casualty other than "killed in action" who has incurred an injury due to an external agent or cause. The term encompasses all kinds of wounds and other injuries incurred in action, whether there is a piercing of the body, as in a penetrating or perforated wound, or none, as in the confused wound; all fractures, burns, blast concussions, all effects of biological and chemical warfare agents, the effects of exposure to ionizing radiation or any other destructive weapon or agent.

Writ of *Certiorari*

It is a writ issuing to the judges or officer of inferior courts, and commanding them to certify and return the record of a matter, *e.g.*, a conviction or order, pending before them, to the end that more sure and speedy justice may be done. If the conviction or order of the inferior court is found to be bad in law, it will be quashed.

Writ of *Habeas Corpus*

It is constitutional remedy for a person wrongfully deprived of his liberty. Any person who is detained in what he conceives to be illegal custody by order of a court-martial or other military authority can apply to a High Court or the Supreme Court for this writ. It is addressed to the person who detains another in custody, and commands him to produce and "have the body" of the prisoner before the court to "undergo and receive" whatever the court considers proper.

Writ of *Mandamus*

The writ of *mandamus* is a command issuing from a Supreme Court directing some person or inferior court to do some particular act which is in the nature of a public duty. There must be a specific legal right to have the act performed, and there must be no other equally convenient and effectual remedy available.

Writ of Quo Warranto

It affords a judicial enquiry in which any person holding an independent substantive public office or franchise or liberty is called upon to show by what right he holds the said office, franchise or liberty; if the enquiry leads to the finding that the holder at the office has no valid title to it, the issue of the writ of quo warranto ousts him from that office.

Writ of Prohibition

This writ issues out of a superior court to any inferior court which concerns itself with any matter not within its jurisdiction, or transgresses the bounds prescribed to it by law. It forbids the inferior court to proceed further in the matter, or to exceed the bound of its jurisdiction, and if the want of jurisdiction in the inferior court be once shown, any person aggrieved by the usurpation of jurisdiction is entitled to the writ as a matter of right.

Writings and Recordings

Consist of letters, words, or numbers, or their equivalent, set down by hand-writing, type-writing, printing, photostating, photographing, magnetic impulse, mechanical or electronic recording, or other form of data compilation. US MRE 1001(1).

Wrong

Any damage or injury, contrary to right, violation of a right or of law, whatever is not right or just. *See* Army Act, section 145(1). To guard against injustice and oppression in the Army, the articles of war clearly point out the mode of redress to every individual in the service, who considers himself wronged by his superiors.

Wrongful Act

A wrongful act is an act forbidden or wrongful by law and is not an improper act. It is any act which unlawfully infringes upon the rights of another.

Wrongfully

Without justification or excuse.

Y

Yeoman

Signifies an officer in the king's house, in the middle place between the searjent and the groom.

Yeomanry

Volunteer cavalry force raised from yeomen.

LEGAL MAXIMS OF RELEVANCE TO MILITARY LAW

ACTA EXTERIORA INDICANT INTERIORA SECRETA.
Acts indicate the intention.

ACTUS CURLE NEMINEM GRAVABIT.
An act of the court shall prejudice no man.

ACTUS DEI NEMINI FACIT INJURIAM.
The law holds no man responsible for the act of God.

CUILIBET IN SUA ARTE PERITO EST CREDENDUM.
Credence should be given to one skilled in his peculiar profession.

DE MINIMIS NON CURAT LEX.
The law does not concern itself about trifles.

DOMUS SUA CUIQUE EST TUTISSIMUM REFUGIUM.
Every man's house is his castle.

EL DOLO MALO NON ORITUR ACTIO.
A right of action cannot arise out of fraud.

EXPRESSIO UNIUS EST EXCLUSIO ALTERIUS.
The express mention of one thing implies the exclusion of another.

FALSA DEMONSTRATIO NON NOCET.
More false description does not vitiate, if there be sufficient certainty as to the object.

IN PRESENTIA MAJORIS CESSAT POTENTIA MINORIS.
In presence of the greater, the power of the inferior ceases.

INTER ARMA SILENT LEGES.
During war, the law is silent.

JURA NOVIT CURIA.
It is for the court to know the law.

LEGES POSTERIORES PRIORES CONTRARIAS ABROGANT.
Later laws repeal earlier laws inconsistent therewith.

NEMO DEBET BIS VEXARI PRO UNA ET EADEM CAUSA.
It is a rule of law that a man shall not be twice vexed for one and the same cause.

NEMO DEBET ESSE JUDEX IN PROPRIA SUA CAUSA.
No man can be judge in his own cause.

NEMO TENETUR SEIPSUM ACCUSARE.

No man can be compelled to criminate himself.

NOVA CONSTITUTIO FUTURIS FORMAM IMPONERE DEBET, NON PRETERITIS.

A new law ought to be prospective, not retrospective, in its operations.

NULLUS COMMODUM CAPERE DE INJURIA SUA PROPRIA.

No man can take advantage of his own wrong.

OMNE MAJUS CONTINET IN SE MINUS.

The greater contains the less.

OMNIA PRESUMUNTUR CONTRA SPOLIATOREM.

Every presumption is made against a wrong doer.

OMNIA PRESUMUNTUR RITE ET SOLENNITER ESSE ACTA.

All acts are presumed to have been done rightly and regularly.

OMNIS RATIHABITIO RETROTRAHITUR ET MANDATO PRIORI EQUIPARATUR.

A subsequent ratification has a retrospective effect, and is equivalent to a prior command.

RES IPSA LOQUITUR.

The thing speaks for itself.

RESPONDEAT SUPERIOR.

Let the principal be held responsible.

SIC UTERE TUO UT ALIENUM NON LEDAS.

Enjoy your own property in such a manner as not to injure that of another person.

TERRAE DOMINIUM FINITUR, UBI FINITUR ARMORUM VIS.

The dominium of the land ends where the range of fire arm ends.

UBI JUS IBI REMEDIUM.

There is no wrong without a remedy.

VIGILANTIBUS, NON DORMIENTIBUS, JURA SUBVENIUNT.

The laws assist those who are vigilant, not those who sleep over their rights.

VOLENTI NON FIT INJURIA.

Damage suffered by consent is not a cause of action.

NOTES

NOTES

NOTES

NOTES

NOTES